When we think of prison, how often do we think of rape? The general consensus being, if a person committed a crime, they deserve whatever they get once inside. But does someone, especially a young offender, deserve to be robbed of their humanity, their autonomy over their own body? Male prison rape is a harsh reality willfully ignored by both prison culture— guards, warden, staff, other inmates—and society itself. How can a prisoner ever expect to be rehabilitated in such an unforgiving environment? *82189* is a horrific document, and it achieves the nearly impossible: As I read it, I came to empathize with a man who willfully made others suffer. It is an important work, the unique record of a man who was both perpetrator and victim. *82189* rightly deserves to become a classic in that most elusive of literatures: redemption through unwarranted suffering. This is humanity, writ large. Thank god it isn't you.

— James Nulick, author of *The Moon Down to Earth*

82189

Confessions of a Prison Bitch

HENRY BELLOWS

Commentary by Mikita Brottman

NINE-BANDED
BOOKS

Published by

Nine-Banded Books
PO Box 1862
Charleston, WV 25327
U.S.A.

NineBandedBooks.com

Special thanks to Anita Dalton, James Nulick, and Peter Sotos.

Cover design by Kevin I. Slaughter

CONTENTS

INTRODUCTION

MIKITA BROTTMAN

82189 IS AN UNFINISHED MEMOIR; the author, who now assumes the pen-name Henry Bellows, died in prison in 2018, at the age of 71. Like many lifers, he'd settled into a kind of basic, low-level contentment. For the last twenty years, he hadn't used tobacco, alcohol, or drugs. He'd held down a basic prison job, and his record was infraction-free. But a lifetime behind bars had taken its toll, and his health had been frail for a while.

Four or five years before he died, Henry Bellows had been a student in a literature class I taught in the Maryland prison where he'd been an inmate for the last fifteen years. He began to write his memoir after the class read *Ham on Rye*, Charles Bukowski's bleak, blunt semi-autobiographical account of his miserable coming-of-age. To Bellows, *Ham on Rye* was a revelation. He told me it was the first book he'd read that didn't gloss over the true facts of life. In a similar way, without compromise or censorship, he wanted to write about his sexual history, both inside and outside prison.[1]

---

1   A few edits have been made to the memoir for the purposes of clarity, and names have been changed for reasons of privacy; otherwise, the narrative remains unaltered.

Bellows found the process of writing absorbing, and sent me new pages whenever he could (usually through a third party, since we weren't supposed to communicate outside the prison classroom). Sometimes they'd be handwritten, but most of the time they were typed, with annotations and revisions in pen. At first, Bellows struggled to find the right style for his story. While he admired Bukowski's pared-down, disconnected sentences, he wanted to tell his own tale in a more straightforward, linear way. However, he died before he was able to complete the memoir, and what remains is raw and patchy. The only complete part is the first section "Defective Delinquent" (a phrase coined in 1910 by the eugenicist movement to describe a new class of "feeble-minded," "intractable," or "emotionally unbalanced" criminals and other "degenerate types"). In this chapter, Bellows tells his story retrospectively, in the voice of a damaged, confused young man struggling to put up a brave front against the world.

In the sections that follow, the narrative is more fragmentary; the voice is that of a jaded and increasingly hostile adult. Here, Bellows recaptures his experiences in bold strokes. He'd intended to go back through these parts and fill in the details, but he never got the chance. Still, from the first chapter, we can get a sense of the kinds of elaborations he would have made. The narrator of "Defective Delinquent" has an impressive visual memory for male-oriented objects: his baseball glove and bat, his father's drop-cloth, Zippo lighter, and station wagon. The latter is a lethal object of fascination which the young Bellows can't seem to leave alone.

Cars are objects that matter to him. His father drives "a 1955 Chevy station wagon with ladder racks on the roof." He is taken to Beaumont in "a brand-new, black, four-door Ford with no door or window knobs in the back seat." When his parents come to visit him there, his father has a new car, "a black 1958 Chevy Impala with white wall tires—a popular model at the time."

From reading through Bellows' judicial records and accounts of his crimes in contemporary newspapers, I have no doubt that his narrative is reliable. He wasn't the type to grandstand, exaggerate, or seek attention. Even if he hadn't died before the memoir was published, he would still have wanted to it remain anonymous, partly because his victims are still living, but also because he didn't want his whole life to be judged by the fifteen years covered in the chapters of this book. He committed no more crimes after 1978, when he was sent to prison for life, aged 27. For the next forty years, in various state prisons, he lived the same type of unremarkable, humdrum life as the rest of us.

The kind of treatment Bellows received as a child at the hands of the state has been well documented elsewhere. The sadistic regime of abuse carried out at the Beaumont Juvenile Correction Center—formerly the Virginia Industrial School for Boys—has been corroborated by both inmates and visitors (alumnae include serial killer Henry Lee Lucas, who spent the best part of a year there). Beaumont, which closed in 2017, was plagued by overcrowding. There were reports of violence, humiliation, excessive isolation and other forms of maltreatment.[2] The lack of educational facilities meant that many boys, like Bellows, spent a good portion of their time working on Beaumont's farm. The following, from a 1978 West Virginia Supreme Court opinion is a description of some of these punitive practices:

> Inmates…were punished by confinement in small, windowless steel-walled cells. …The cells are about four feet wide, eight feet long and eight feet high. Youths placed in them were allowed to wear only their undershorts. "Floor time" was a punishment whereby the inmate apparently was required to stand stiffly in one position for several hours each day without talking. "Bench time" was a punishment that required the inmate to sit in a specified location with arms crossed for several hours each day and for several days without talking or moving. Mace…was freely used by staff upon inmates whose behavior did not suit staff requirements.[3]

Even as late as 2014, things had changed very little. Andrew Block, Director of the Virginia Department of Juvenile Justice from 2014 to 2019, described the residential units at Beaumont as

> stale and austere places… What little natural light there was came from small skylights in the ceiling, but the illumination from these openings was negligible. The walls

2   Arnold, Michael, "Crowding, Violence Plague Youth Detention Centers," *Washington Post*, September 14, 1993.

3   242 S.E.2d 907 (1978), *State of West Virginia ex rel. K. W. and C. W. v. Stewart Werner, Commissioner of Corrections, etc., et al.* Nos. 14002, 14003, 14051 and 14052. Supreme Court of Appeals of West Virginia. January 31, 1978.

were cinder-block and painted white. The floors were concrete and the lights dim and fluorescent. Each kid had a cell that was behind a heavy, steel door. The cells themselves were equally stark, with a concrete bed with a thin mattress and pillow, a shiny metal sink and toilet, a slit of a frosted window, and naked white walls with those same fluorescent lights.[4]

By the time he left Beaumont at the age of 12, Bellows had suffered many violent beatings at the hands of his father, a convicted rapist. He'd overheard his father sexually abusing his mother at night. He'd been molested by a babysitter. He'd learned to drink, smoke, drive, steal cars and break into houses. He'd been victimized by older youths. He'd spent six months in juvenile detention. Even before his gang-rape initiation, it's difficult to imagine him growing up to live a law-abiding life.

His memoir is uncomfortably split between two perspectives, and it's unclear exactly how aware Bellows was of the relationship between his childhood treatment and his adult behavior. For readers on the outside, of course, it's easy to join the dots. The terrible violence inflicted on the child by his father seems arbitrary and unmotivated. Equally capricious is the father's impulse to buy his son the gift of a brand-new bicycle, seemingly out of the blue. Bellows' first stirrings of sexual arousal (he calls them "funny feelings") are directed towards his mother. Although he sympathizes with

4   Andrew Block, "First Days: Tragedy and Transformation in Juvenile Justice," *Crime Story*, August 16 2019, https://crimestory.com/2019/08/16/first-days-tragedy-and-transformation-in-juvenile-justice/ accessed Jan 22, 2021.

her cries of pain at night, they also provoke what appears to be his first nocturnal emission, and he soon begins to feel a heightened sense of erotic excitement in response to other people's suffering. Scaring Joanie, the babysitter, makes him feel good. He enjoys her "rubbing and sucking" him, but his powerlessness in the situation makes it impossible for him to get aroused. When he gets older, he becomes a Peeping Tom, and while he likes to look at girls and women, he feels contempt for their passivity. Out of the blue, he finds himself hurling a racial epithet at a girl who reminds him of Joanie. After his younger brother is born, he stops caring that his mother is being sexually victimized by his father. He complains about his own physical weakness. "I failed in every area of masculinity. I had no facial hair, no pubic hair, and only peach fuzz on my arms and legs. I was slim, and my arms were small. I didn't measure up." Disdainful of his slight, feminine body, he learns to compensate by identifying with the aggressor.

Three years later, cops lock this "scared," "skinny little kid" in a D.C. jail overnight, in an open dormitory filled with adult male inmates. At fourteen, he's barely reached puberty; he hasn't even begun to masturbate. Surely, as Bellows states, the law enforcement officers must have known what they were doing. The all-night gang rape, flatly described, is a turning point in the narrative. It's the story of his life in miniature. Around three or four in the morning, after being beaten, raped and defiled by—in Bellows' estimation—between "forty and fifty" men, he is "befriended" (and pimped out) by Tangerine, whose advice he takes to heart. "[I]f I didn't want them to hurt me, I had to act as though I liked what they were doing." His resistance is broken down, and he stops struggling. In short, Bellows is turned out.

The legal definition of sexual abuse in prisons does not include "consensual activity between inmates," a definition which implies that consent is a straightforward matter of simply saying "yes" or "no." There's no question that gang-rapes like the one described here frequently take place in jails and prisons, and the fact that Bellows eventually comes to accept and even embrace his role as a "prison bitch" shows how vexed the question of "consent" really is. In her 2006 article "Sexual Punishments," law professor Alice Ristroph reminds us that "sex in prison is in many ways a peculiar product of the carceral environment, and far more complicated than the paradigmatic account of prison rape. That account posits predator and prey: a cruel, sadistic perpetrator who manipulates or violently overpowers a vulnerable victim."[5] As Bellows' experience shows us, this is an illusion. "Eventually," writes Bellows, "I became submissive and effeminate, and no one had to threaten me or hurt me in order to have sex with them." Later, he explains, "it took a while, but I learned to like having sex with men, and then, at some point, I became addicted to it."

U.S. prisons don't distribute condoms on the grounds that rape is against the law, and "consensual" sex against the rules, perpetuating the fiction that over two million adult men spend a significant part of their lives—in many cases, their entire adulthood—abstaining from sexual contact

---

5   Alice Ristroph, "Sexual Punishments," 15 *Columbia Journal of Gender and Law* 139 (2006), 141.

altogether. Of course, sex (in various forms, with different degrees and measures of consent) happens all the time in prison, partly because there's not much else to do, and partly because inmates, like anyone else, crave affection and intimacy. Mostly, however, it happens because for many prisoners, the body's innate, freely-generated pleasure is the only form of pleasure they have left, and because sexual contact is a reliable source of affirmation and validation in an otherwise bleak and empty life. Female prisoners became pregnant in concentration camps, after all.

Could Bellows have stopped or prevented any of the sexual abuse he suffered in prison? Attempting to do so would, most likely, have only have led to further violence. In my experience, complaints about treatment in prison are pointless. The Prison Litigation Reform Act requires that inmates exhaust all "internal grievance procedures" before taking their issue to the courts. In practical terms, these in-house "investigations" are almost always a dead end. Bureaucratic procedures are often deliberately opaque, and usually impossible for an ordinary inmate to follow. Prison administrators protect one another from inmate complaints or accusations through misrepresentation or intimidation. Guards, if not perpetrators themselves, soon learn to turn a blind eye. Prison guard unions are one of the strongest forces in American labor.

The courts decry sexual violence in correctional facilities, yet one of the reasons for its prevalence is their reluctance to get involved in what happens in prisons. When I first started teaching inmates, I was surprised to see the PREA (Prison

Rape Elimination Act) hotline number stamped on every wall. It was difficult for me to imagine how a prisoner experiencing sexual abuse could be helped by a call to a national "rape hotline" given the culture of retaliation in prisons, not to mention the inmates' limited access to the phones (which are very public). After a while, however, I came to see that the printing the PREA number on the wall merely ensured the prison was in legal compliance. It was a symbolic gesture only, not a way to change things. As Alice Ristroph explains, PREA is a "mostly hortatory statute, seemingly intended primarily to express condemnation of physically violent sexual aggression" that "fails either to recognize the complicated forms of sexual coercion or to address the underlying structural problems with the prison."[6]

Rape counseling advocates reassure male victims that the body's reactions can't be controlled, and that a "purely physiological response" of erection and ejaculation can occur in the "absence of healthy sexual pleasure" (which surely begs the question of what exactly "counts" as "healthy sexual pleasure"). The fact is, rape victims can and sometimes do experience "sexual pleasure" despite the terrible nature of their ordeal. The sex drive is rebellious, colonizing, paradoxical, and inconvenient. Humiliation can be eroticized. Physical pain can be a way of escaping, at least temporarily, from the boundaries of the self. Unwanted sexual experiences, repeated often enough, can—unconsciously, unintentionally—eventually become pleasurable. The most common internet porn search terms ("stepmom," "rape," "teen," "gangbang")

---

6   175–6 Ibid.

invoke sexual scenarios that are socially prohibited. Taboos, after all, are directed against our strongest desires.

In the context of prison, intimidation and consent are almost impossible to define. Prison is an inherently coercive environment, and inmates have no autonomy or freedom of choice. "Being a prison bitch was no different from being a slave, or a prisoner-of-war," writes Bellows. "If I'd resisted, somebody would have killed me long ago." It takes years, but Bellows begins to associate sexual assault with attention, with feeling wanted and desired, and then with safety and trust. By "becoming a woman," as he puts it[7]—in other words, by embracing his abjection—he overcomes his fears of abandonment, his emotional loneliness, his inability to trust adults in intimate relations, his self-contempt. Later still, he starts to associate giving oral sex to men with feelings of well-being, assurance, and pleasure:

> I haven't really tried to analyze it, but I know that the thing that gives me the most pleasure in the world is sucking dick. I really don't know why this is, but it reminds me of how a baby is comforted by sucking and chewing on a pacifier. I think my love of dick isn't just sexual. At some level, it also gives me a feeling of comfort and safety.

Some may find it surprising that a man who, in his own words, "preferred sex with men," should go on to rape women, but the second part of the story, unfortunately,

---

7 In this light, it is perhaps no coincidence that at San Quentin, according to Bellows, the cons' favorite Johnny Cash hit was "A Boy Named Sue."

follows naturally from the first. Many studies have shown that abuse perpetrated by a male caregiver is strongly associated with subsequent hypersexuality and aggression in adult male sex offenders.[8] After a cross country crime-spree leads to a three-and-a-half year stretch in San Quentin and Soledad, Bellows returns to Virginia with the "driving ambition" to "create a new identity," to go from being "a mindless jailhouse bitch" to "a real man." In order to do so, he says, "I needed to forget my past," but, whether he's conscious of it or not, his past continues to direct his actions. When his second wife rejects him, he breaks into a house and rapes a mother and daughter. The description of rapes in this narrative—those Bellows experiences, as well as those he commits—are difficult to read, but however unpalatable, these things happened. There's a shocking honesty in Bellows' account of how much pleasure it gave him to finally assert sexual control over another person. To him, it is a victory. "It felt wonderful!"

He commits his first rape only seven years after being raped for the first time himself, but Bellows draws no connection between the pain and humiliation he suffered in the D.C. jail and the distress and degradation he inflicts on his first two victims. On the contrary, he enjoys the rape so

---

8   See, for example, Ashley Jesperson, Martin L. Lalumière, & Michael C. Seto, "Sexual abuse history among adult sex offenders and non-sex offenders: a meta-analysis," *Child Abuse and Neglect*, March 33(3) 2009:179–92; Raymond A. Knight and Judith E. Sims-Knight, "The developmental antecedents of sexual coercion against women: testing alternative hypotheses with structural equation modeling," *Annual of New York Academy of Science*, June 2003, 989: 72–85; discussion 144-53; Jill S. Levenson and Melissa D. Grady, "Preventing Sexual Abuse: Perspectives of Minor-Attracted Persons About Seeking Help," *Sexual Abuse*, Dec 31(8) 2019: 991–1013.

much that he starts breaking into houses looking for other women to assault. His description of these sadistic attacks is the most disturbing part of the memoir, mainly because he's able to recapture his excitement so convincingly. He feels no sympathy for his victims and says nothing about what the experience must have been like for them, apart from wondering whether or not they had bad dreams. Instead, he recounts graphic details of the assaults in a tone of smug triumph.

Notably, this memoir contains no references to treatment, only punishment. Today, a child in Bellows' situation would almost certainly be prescribed medication for ADHD (he recalls being unable to sit still long enough to play board games), and, no doubt, for depression, anxiety, and probably bipolar disorder as well (although it's hard to say whether he would have agreed to take medication if it had been prescribed, and whether it would have helped him if he did). Although it wasn't widely available in the 1970s, sex-drive-lowering medication (sometimes called "chemical castration") would almost certainly have helped him—his criminal behavior, after all, is driven by his compelling and powerful biological craving for sex. But treatment is offered only to the mentally ill, and the desire to rape is seen as an indication of criminality, not of mental illness. "Coercive paraphilia," or rape fetishism, has been continually rejected by the committee of psychiatrists who decide what conditions will be included in the *Diagnostic and Statistical Manual of Mental Disorders*. As a result, rapists, like pedophiles and others with socially stigmatized paraphilias, receive long prison sentences, not sympathy, psychiatric hospitalization, or therapeutic interventions.

Bellows had no opportunity for therapy of any kind, in fact, until five or six years into the life sentence he received for rape in 1976. In the early 1980s, he was sent to Patuxent Institution, an experimental maximum-security prison in Maryland which accepted violent "defective delinquents" from other state prisons and attempted to reform them through psychotherapy. The regime at Patuxent changed over the years, according to various waves and fashions in penal philosophy. When Bellows was an inmate there, the institution used a "graded tier system" in which an inmate progressed through four levels of rehabilitation and increased privileges, effecting a gradual return to society through 12-hour furloughs, then daytime jobs, and finally parole.

Bellows made "leave status" at Patuxent in 1986, ten years after receiving his life sentence, and maintained his status until 1988. During those two years, he left Patuxent and went out into the community approximately 350 times. Every Monday, along with other inmates, he worked with boys at a local middle school; on Wednesdays, he went to a local courthouse, where he worked with at-risk kids who were on probation. On Fridays, he went to another middle school where he worked with a different group of juveniles. He also gave "scared straight"-type talks at various local community associations, schools, and churches. He wasn't allowed to drink or use drugs during these furloughs, and he never did. "I was too scared to drink or take anything," he told me. "They always pissed me every time I went out."[9] At the time, he believed each successful community visit was bringing him closer to parole, but the furlough program in Patuxent was revoked on December 1, 1988 after a number of high-profile inmates on work release fled and committed further crimes. The most notable of these was Willie Horton, who was arrested in Maryland while on furlough from a prison in Massachusetts. Since 1988, Bellows has not left the prison grounds.

In person, Henry Bellows was—as might be expected after forty years in prison—cynical, closed-off, jaded and mistrusting. "Today it's hard for me to find anything that will make me laugh out loud," he writes. His prose, while smooth and easy to read, has little life or spirit. Some people will find it difficult to sympathize with him, given his lack of remorse. But he has enough insight into what other people called his "criminal behavior" to see it for what it really was, "just me thrashing around like a wounded animal, in pain and out of control." As fellow human beings, we should try to see his actions in the same way. After all, it's too easy to tell ourselves that this is someone else's story, not our own.

---

9   I.e.. subjected him to a urine test.

82189

Beaumont Boys School

1

DEFECTIVE DELINQUENT

I FEEL CERTAIN that if abortion had been legal, there'd be no story to tell.

My father met and married my mother right after being discharged from the army. Like so many baby boomers, I was an unexpected arrival.

Dad drove a 1955 Chevy station wagon with ladder racks on the roof and the word "Decorators" painted on the side. Despite his many faults, my father was a hard worker, but since he could barely read or write, my mother took down dictation and made up his contracts. I'd sit in the living room and listen to them at the dining room table talking about the jobs he had to do, and how much he charged for each one. It's the only time I can remember them really talking to each other. It was certainly the only time Mom had the upper hand.

At first, we lived in a series of old, run-down houses that Dad would fix up and sell. Each time, he'd invest the profits in a better house. After five moves and five houses, we moved into the simple, two-bedroom white stucco house on Cedar Lane. I never felt safe or happy in that house.

By the time I turned eight, I'd grown introverted and shy. I was an only child, lacking in confidence and social skills; moving from place to place so often had made it impossible for me to make friends. At school, I was always a loner, sometimes acting out in class just to get attention. I was never a good student, but somehow, I managed to get by.

My father drank whiskey, and I never felt safe around him. He could be perfectly calm one minute, the next he'd be yelling violently about something as trivial as the television being too loud.

One day I brought a couple of my Little League teammates home to throw a baseball around. My father saw us and came outside.

"If that ball hits my house," he yelled, "I'll break someone's fucking arm!"

I was so embarrassed I couldn't speak.

"Let's go," said one of the other boys, and we walked the half-mile back to the school field. It would be ten years before I'd invite anyone to my house again.

On Sundays, we all got dressed up to go and visit our relatives. Dad cleaned the station wagon inside and out, but when I got in the back seat, I could always smell paint and varnish. If either Mom or I mentioned the smell, the day was ruined. Dad would launch into an angry tirade about how hard he worked and all the bills he had to pay.

When my dad wanted to go squirrel hunting, we'd visit my grandfather. He had over a hundred acres of property, and I'd get to roam the woods while he and my dad were hunting squirrels. There was a lot of land at my grandfather's place, but not much else, not even a paved driveway leading to the house, just a bumpy dirt road and several tumble-down shacks that Grandfather rented out to the people who worked for him. None of the houses had indoor plumbing, not even Grandfather's. They all had outhouses and cast iron, wood-burning stoves. I could never tell if my grandfather was cheap, stubborn, crazy, or all three. With all his money and property, he still used a nasty smelling outhouse, with flies buzzing round your ass. I'd rather just walk into the woods and squat.

Sometimes we went to visit Uncle Walt and Aunt Peggy, who lived in a neighborhood development where all the houses looked alike. Each had an open driveway leading to a two-car garage. Uncle Walt didn't say much, but he liked cooking on the outside grill with my dad. Aunt Peggy was always kind to me. My two cousins were named Johnny and Laura. Laura was pretty, and around my age. Whenever I saw her I got these funny feelings. She was the only person who made me feel like this apart from Mom.

One Sunday, we were over at Uncle Walt and Aunt Peggy's and I found myself alone with Laura in her bedroom. We'd only been there for a minute or two when I heard Aunt Irene and Mom coming to find us.

"We shouldn't leave these two alone together," said Aunt Peggy. Several years later, I'd find out why.

Since I couldn't be alone with Laura, I went outside to see how dinner was coming along. Uncle Walt and my father were having a loud argument.

"Get your mother, we're going home!" yelled Dad.

"Please don't go, Billy," pleaded Aunt Irene, but my father's mind was made up. We left without even eating dinner. As we drove away, I waved to Laura who watched us drive away.

As we pulled up in front of our house, Mom asked, "What are we going to eat?"

"I'm hungry!" I complained.

My father brought the car to a stop, turned off the engine, and turned around. Suddenly I saw a flash. There was an explosion in my forehead. My father had struck me, and hard.

"What are you doing?" screamed Mom. She pulled me out of the car, dragged me into the house, and locked us both in the hallway bathroom. Examining my head, she found a small bump over my right eye. I was in pain, and frightened of what Dad might do to me next. But at the same time, it felt good to know Mom really cared about me. My father was storming around the house, cursing and threatening her. When she heard him going into the bedroom, she opened the bathroom door and we ran out through the kitchen.

By then it was dark outside. We sat under the oak tree under my parents' bedroom window.

"If it weren't for you, I'd leave him," said Mom.

After about an hour, when she was sure Dad was asleep, Mom took me inside and put me to bed. The next day, I knew, they'd act as if nothing had happened, the bump on my forehead gone. But my mother's words continued to bother me. It was for my sake, I realized, that she was putting up with my father's violence. Now he was turning on me.

The next night, about half an hour after Mom had gone to bed, I crept into the living room and took down my dad's wallet from the fireplace mantle. I didn't count how much money there was, but I knew it was at least a hundred dollars.

I put it in my pocket and left.

•

SLOWLY AND QUIETLY, I closed the aluminum storm door behind me. Standing on the porch outside the kitchen, I paused to listen for sounds inside the house. Everything was silent.

I walked to the end of the drive, and began walking up Cedar Lane. Each time I saw car headlights I got scared and hid, which was crazy. No one would know I was missing for several hours, yet I was already acting like an escaped criminal.

Cedar Lane merged into another road at the District Firehouse, which sat off by itself in a clearing. My father drove an ambulance there as a volunteer. He wasn't on call tonight, but I still didn't want to be seen. I kept walking. I figured I could make the two miles to Route 7 in about 20 minutes. Once there, I could either head left, toward West Virginia, or right, toward Washington, DC.

At the junction, I came to a gas station, a truck stop, a small store and a hamburger joint. Everything was closed. There was a coke machine, but I didn't have any coins. The bathroom at the gas station was locked, so I took a piss on the ground.

Several wrecked cars were parked at the back of the gas station. I got in the back seat of the one furthest from the road, a '53 Chevy. There were at least four or five hours left before daylight, and my adrenalin was no longer keeping me going; I fell asleep right away.

The sound of a barking dog woke me up. First, I thought I was dreaming; then I remembered where I was, and how I got there. Filled with fear, I reached into my pocket to feel the bills. They were still there. That took away some of my anxiety.

I was hungry and thirsty, and I needed to take a shit. By this time the bathroom was unlocked, so I went inside, locked the door, and used the toilet. Then I washed my hands, drank some water from the sink, and left.

I walked into the hamburger joint and sat on one of the stools at the counter. I noticed the clock; it was 9:15.

"What can I get you?"

The trucker at the end of the counter was eating scrambled eggs on toast. I thought about breakfast for a couple of seconds, then I ordered a hamburger and a chocolate milk shake.

"What do you want on your hamburger?" the lady asked.

"Everything," I said. I'd never ordered my own food before, so I didn't know what else to say.

As I ate, I began to think about my mother. Was she worried about me? What would my dad do if he found me? After finishing my hamburger, I went back to the junkyard and got back in the old wrecked Chevy. I stayed there until about 4.30, then I went and bought a Coke and decided to see if I could get a ride with one of the truck drivers. One guy told me he was going to Charlestown West Virginia, to the

30

racetrack, and said I should get up into the cab of the truck. I sat there for a while, then looked down, and there was my dad's face staring at me from inside his station wagon.

Apparently, he'd been out to look for me and given the lady in the hamburger joint his number in case she saw me again. The trucker had just been keeping me waiting while they called my dad. He was a great actor, and could put on a face appropriate for any situation. He thanked the lady and the trucker politely for their help.

The ride home took less than ten minutes, but it seemed at least an hour. My dad said nothing until we turned into the driveway.

Then he said, "Go inside."

I opened the front door and my mother was standing in the middle of the living room. I'd never seen my mother shed a single tear, but this day she came close, rushing over to me and putting her arms around my neck.

"Where's the money?" said my dad.

I reached into my pocket and pulled out the bills and change. I'd spent less than a dollar. He wanted to know what I'd spent it on.

"The money doesn't matter, Billy," said my mother. "He's home safe."

For a few days after I got back, the house was quiet. There was no arguing and not much talking. Then, without warning, everything started again—the drinking, the anger, and the threats. I started to feel as though all their fights were due to me. I also felt my father wouldn't have come after me if I hadn't taken the money, and I realized that if I ran away again, I'd need a plan, a place to go, and a way to get there. And next time, I wouldn't trust anybody.

Shortly after that, my mother got pregnant, and my father stopped pushing and hitting her for a while. When my baby brother Buddy was around a month old, the violence started again. I stayed away from the house as much as possible. I became more involved with sports, especially Little League Baseball. Our team didn't win very often, and nobody came to see me play, but it was the best thing in my life at that time. I always liked playing at our school's field, about half a mile away. If I could hit the ball with the fat part of my bat, I could make an easy home run over the left field fence. I was tied with Joey Duke for the most home runs, and I badly wanted to win.

One Saturday, my dad told me he wanted the leaves in the front yard raked before I could leave for the game. He had these large drop cloths that he used to cover floors and furniture when he was painting houses, and he showed me how to spread them out, rake the piles of leaves on to them, then drag them out to the back yard. We had a new bamboo rake in the shed that was light and easy to use, so I raked the leaves into piles then went into the house to get dressed for the game. As luck would have it, I was leaving the house with my glove and bat just as my father was pulling into the driveway.

"Where do you think you're going?" he said. I could see the anger in his face.

"We have a game at school."

"No, you don't. You're not going anywhere until those leaves are in the back yard.

"I've raked them already. I'll move them when I get back."

"No," he said.

The anger swelled in my body. Baseball was all that mattered to me. The games were the only time and place where I mattered, where it made a difference whether I was there or not. For the first time, my fear took a back seat to my anger, and I realized I was becoming just like my father. He got out of the car and came towards me, pulling off his belt. I wanted to run, but my legs wouldn't respond. He grabbed my wrist, and I dropped my glove and bat. He started beating me with the belt, and each time the blow landed, it felt like I'd been hit by a rock. Every time he hit me, I managed to pull him forward a couple of feet, but he wouldn't let me get away. I thought he was never going to stop. He beat the whole left side of my body from my lower back to my ankle. By the time he'd finished beating me, I'd managed to pull him all the way round the house and back to the driveway again. When it was over, he told me to go to my room, and forget about the ball game.

By this time, my mother had stopped trying to intervene; she was too busy protecting Buddy. After the violence was over, she'd come and bandage my cuts and welts. "You should do what your father tells you," she'd say.

I decided I'd run away again as soon as baseball season was over. At the end of the season, I won a trophy for being the team's Most Valuable Player. Roy Seivers of the Washington Senators presented it to me, and Mom came to see me. It was the one time I accomplished anything to make a parent proud. However, by then, she'd stopped protecting me from my dad, and I'd stopped caring how my dad treated her.

•

MOM LIKED TO DANCE, and the District Firehouse held dances every Saturday night. During her pregnancy, however, she couldn't go. Not long after my brother was born, mom and dad had their first night out in a long time. I was nine years old.

I lounged on the couch, bored. I turned on the TV, even though there was nothing I wanted to watch.

"Keep the noise down. The baby's sleeping," Mom reminded me. It was hard for me to accept I had a new kid brother.

Moments later, Dad walked into the room with a colored girl.

"This is Joanie," he said, not meeting my eye. The girl looked around eighteen. I stared at her. Westville Elementary was still segregated; almost everyone I knew was white.

I could hear my parents talking quietly in the kitchen. Finally, they seemed ready to leave.

"You've got the number at the firehouse. Call me if anything goes wrong," said Mom, as she went to check on the baby one last time.

"Stay off the phone in case we want to check in," said Dad.

Their car backed out of the driveway, and I peered through the curtains to watch them leave.

"What are you doing?" asked Joanie.

"I don't know." Being alone with her made me a little nervous.

She changed the channel to a movie. I lay down on the couch, and she sat next to me. I was too shy to say anything.

After about an hour, the phone rang in the kitchen. We both got up at the same time.

"I got it!" insisted Joanie, and picked up the phone. "Hello, Mrs. B," she said. "Everything's fine. No, he's watching TV."

I heard her hang up, but before long she was on the phone again, talking in a different voice. She talked for a long time.

Several minutes passed and Joanie was still on the phone. I guess she'd been waiting for Mom to call so she could gossip with her friends. I went into the kitchen, opened the icebox and grabbed a Coke. As I pried open the top, the bottle slipped out of my hands, and soda spilled all over the floor.

"Hold on," said Joanie to whoever she was talking to, and covered the receiver with her hand. Then she said, "Clean up that mess or I'll tell your mom!"

"If you do," I said, "I'll tell my dad you were on the phone all night."

My threat scared her. Quickly, she said goodbye to her friend and hung up the phone. Then she cleaned up the Coke.

I went back to the couch, drank the rest of the soda, put the empty bottle on the table then lay down to watch the movie.

After Joanie finished cleaning the kitchen floor, she came over to the couch sat down next to me, then bent over and tried to kiss me. I put my arms up to stop her.

"What's the matter, baby?" she said.

I didn't want to kiss her, but I didn't know what to say. I couldn't understand what she was doing. This was my first sexual experience.

Suddenly, I felt her hand against my stomach. I froze. Her hand moved under my T-shirt and slid inside the elastic waistband of my pants. I was too embarrassed to move. Joanie pushed her hand further down.

"Just lie still. You'll soon feel good," she said.

I'd never been touched this way before, and I had to admit, it did feel good.

"Do you like it?" asked Joanie, continuing to rub and stroke. "Does it feel good?"

I tried to speak, but the words stuck in my mouth.

She began to pull my pants down. I wanted her to stop, but I was too embarrassed to speak. The next thing I knew, she was licking and kissing my dick, stopping occasionally to put it in her mouth and suck on it. I just lay there, helpless, not knowing what to do. So many different things were going through my head. The rubbing and sucking felt good, but I didn't like feeling powerless. When I'd threatened to tell my dad about her using the phone, she'd been scared, and it had felt good. I had the upper hand. Now, however, she had total control, and I was too frightened to ask her to stop.

Finally, after what seemed like forever, she stopped sucking, straightened up, and sighed.

"You're too young, baby," she said. "One day, you'll be like your daddy."

I said nothing, but her words stayed with me. What did she mean? Had she sucked my father's dick the way she sucked mine, or did she just mean I'd grow into a man one day, like my dad?

Relieved the ordeal was over, I pretended to fall asleep, and Joanie covered me with a blanket. When Mom and Dad came home, I said goodbye to Joanie and went to bed. Dad drove her home. I only saw her once more, and that was two years later, at the Westville Country Store. We looked at each other, but neither of us spoke.

A few days later, I had another ego-crushing experience. I was walking up Cedar Lane toward school, and I saw a bunch of guys hanging out by the basketball court. I recognized a couple of them from the baseball team; they were with two older guys, age twelve or thirteen, who I'd never seen before. Always hoping to meet other kids, especially older ones, I decided to go over and see what was going on.

The two older guys were bragging about their girlfriends, and all the things they'd done with them. At nine, despite Joanie, I knew nothing about girls. The only person I'd ever kissed was my mom, and the only person I'd seen naked was my baby brother, when my mom was changing his diaper. In fact, I was surprised she let me see him; Mom was pretty old-fashioned about things like that. Once, when we were visiting family in West Virginia, I walked in on my aunt breastfeeding my little baby cousin, and I remember my mom insisting she cover herself up ("That's not for young boys to see!"). She always locked the bathroom door, even when I was the only other person at home. It always felt so strange to hear the click of the lock. Oddly enough, when I got older, I started to do the same thing.

I didn't know what fucking was, or how my brother got inside my mom's stomach, but I was curious, and I wanted to find out.

"Hey kid," asked one of the older boys. "What do you know about girls?"

"I know what they like," I said, bluffing.

"Okay, so what do they like, you little shit?"

"They like to have their belly touched and rubbed," I said, thinking about what happened with Joanie on the couch. "They like it when you put your hand in their pants and rub them between their legs."

"What do they have between their legs?"

"You know," I said. "The same thing we got."

For a long time, I wasn't allowed to forget what I'd said. Soon, it felt like everybody at school, and in the neighborhood, knew how stupid I was. Wherever I went, it seemed, everybody made fun of me, even the girls.

At least one thing was going well: my dad had more work than he could handle. He hired more decorators, bought a new panel truck, and was now working most weekends.

"Do you want to ride to work with me tomorrow?" he asked me one Friday at the dinner table. "I'll give you a few dollars if you want to learn how to paint."

"Sure," I said. Baseball season was over, and I had nothing to do.

The job, it turned out, was in a rich neighborhood of McLean, Virginia. Dad showed me how to put paint on the brush and told me to paint two garage doors. It was okay at first, but after a while my arm got tired and I had to stop every few minutes to rest. I was afraid Dad would get angry and yell at me, but he was in a good mood.

"Not bad for your first day," he said, and handed me five dollars.

The next day, Dad drove off in his station wagon, to visit potential customers. During the week, when he was working in the suburbs, people would see the sign and phone number on the side of the station wagon and call him with jobs they needed doing. On Sundays, he'd drive out to their houses, take a look at the work and give them an estimate. He left his new panel truck at home.

This truck fascinated me. That day, while Mom was out back behind the house hanging clothes out to dry, I got in and sat behind the steering wheel. It had a foot floor starter and a stick shift with a clutch. Without thinking, I put my foot on the starter pedal and pushed down hard. The truck jerked forward and the engine started to turn over, though it couldn't start without the ignition key. I took my foot off the starter pedal and pushed down on the clutch. The truck started drifting down the slope of the drive and rolled four or five feet over the grass, where it finally came to a stop.

I was in big trouble. First, I thought about asking Mom to drive it back, but then I remembered she couldn't drive a stick shift. Then I considered running away again, but I didn't have any money or anywhere to go. I didn't want to face my dad, so I decided to sneak next door and hide behind the neighbor's grapevine. From there, I could watch the driveway. My plan was to hide until my dad came home. He didn't get back for a long time. I just hung out quietly under the vine, and after I'd been there for a while, I noticed all the birds and squirrels starting to come out.

I sat there until it started to get dark, and a light went on in the neighbor's house behind me. I didn't know the people who lived there; they'd just bought the house and moved in a couple of months ago. I was curious about them, and moved closer to the window to see if could see inside. Suddenly, car headlights appeared and turned into our driveway. Dad was home.

I watched as he got out of the station wagon, walked up to the truck, and looked in the front door window. He didn't open the door. I expected him to get in and move it back to the driveway, but he just went in the house. I wondered if he even noticed it was parked in a different place.

As soon as I came out of my hiding place, the back light came on, and my mom saw me and yelled for me to come inside. She had no idea what was going to happen.

Dad was waiting for me at the door.

"Have you been in my truck?" he said. "What did you do?"

I didn't say anything, which made him even angrier.

"Go to your room," he said.

•

THROUGH MY BEDROOM WINDOW I could see my dad walking toward the shed where he kept firewood and kindling. I didn't want to see any more, so I turned away from

the window and switched off the lights. I knew he was looking for the biggest, strongest piece of wood he could find.

A few minutes later, my bedroom door opened and the
light came on. I was hit by a wave of fear, and I felt my body
cringing in anticipation of the pain. I was helpless. I cowered
in the corner, wrapping my arms around my head. Then the
blows came, fast and deliberate. Many times, the neighbors
must have heard me yelling for him to stop, but however
loud I cried, it made no difference.

Next morning, my ass and thighs were stinging with welts
and bruises, and my right knee was so swollen I couldn't
walk. Except for taking a long hot bath, I stayed in bed
all day. Mom took care of me, bringing me meals, but she
hardly said a word. Dad worked late into the evening, and
I didn't see him again until the next day, when the swelling
in my knee had gone down enough for me to put my weight
on it. He opened my bedroom door in the morning, when I
was still in bed.

"Get dressed boy, we're going out," he said.

Too scared to ask any questions, I limped out to the truck.
Twenty minutes later, Dad pulled into the parking lot of the
hardware store. He took me to the back, where the lawn-
mowers and wheelbarrows were. Pointing to a row of bicy-
cles, he said, "Pick one."

I didn't know what he meant, and the expression on my
face must have told him so.

"Take a good look at those bikes," he said, "and tell me
which one you like."

I was totally confused. I walked over and looked at the

bikes. Only two were my size: a lightweight, three-speed twenty-six inch English Racer, and a twenty-inch maroon road bike with wide tires, a light on the front, and wire baskets on each side of the back fenders. This one, the less expensive of the two, would be most practical for riding through the woods and trails where we lived, so that was the one I chose. I don't know whether it was guilt or regret that made my father buy me the bike. I didn't ask.

The first time I rode it, I heard someone calling my name. It was Bob, an older boy who lived next door. He asked me if I wanted to make some money selling donuts in the neighborhood.

"This guy comes by our house every Saturday and Sunday morning with fresh donuts," Bob told me. "He'll give you several boxes, and if you sell three boxes, you get a box to sell for yourself."

"Sure," I said. I thought it sounded like an easy way to make money, but I was wrong. People didn't buy as many donuts as I thought they would, and I got into trouble for eating them and giving them away. I didn't make any money that way, and I knew I needed money in case I ever ran away again. There was a newspaper route available in the neighborhood, and I took it.

It was around this time I first started smoking. I knew where my dad kept his whiskey and cigarettes, and when I mentioned this to my friend Vinny—one of the kids from the baseball team—he dared me to steal some. I'd made a vow that I'd never steal money from my mom or dad again, but cigarettes were different. They both smoked Lucky Strikes. If a few went missing from a pack, I figured they'd never notice. The whiskey, however, would be a different story.

I took a handful of cigarettes and rode my bike as fast as I could to Vinny's house, about three miles away. I'd often watched my mom and dad smoking, but I'd never thought to try it myself until Vinny dared me. I wanted to prove I wasn't scared. I made a left off Cedar Lane, into the road where Vinny lived, a dirt path about a mile long leading to a dead end. His house was the one next to last.

"Hey Vinny," I yelled, riding into his front yard. He was in the backyard with his bike upside down, trying to fix his back wheel.

"Hey, come over here and hold my bike," he said.

I laid my bike on the ground (I never used the kick stand), waved to Vinny's mom on the back porch, and went over to give him a hand.

"Did you get it?" he asked, in a low voice.

"I got the Lucky Strikes, that's all."

"No whiskey? You're such a chickenshit!"

I'd looked at the whiskey bottles in the cabinet under the kitchen sink, and they were all almost full.

"I'll get some next time," I said.

We replaced the wheel on his bike, then I followed Vinny to the chicken coop and we went inside. The chickens were all out in the yard. There was chicken shit everywhere.

"Let's light up," he said.

Then I realized I'd forgotten to bring matches.

"Wait here," said Vinny. "I'll see if I can find some."

A few minutes later, he came running back and asked me

for a cigarette. I'd brought nine or ten of them, and I handed one to Vinny. He stuck it in his mouth and pulled out a lighter. "This is my dad's Zippo," he said, lighting the cigarette. "If he knew I'd taken it, he'd beat my ass good." He took a big puff than handed it to me. "Here, your turn."

I felt strange holding a lit cigarette. It almost felt like I was holding a gun. I sucked in the smoke and immediately began coughing. I tried several more times before I could take in the smoke and blow it out without choking on it. We smoked them all, one after another. I started smoking that day, and didn't stop for many years.

One of the families on my paper route had a pretty black dog that looked like a miniature Irish setter. Every day, when I came by to drop off the paper, Sassy would be waiting for me. As soon as she saw me coming, she'd run up to me, her tail wagging, and when I was ready to leave she'd always try to follow me. One day, I learned Sassy's owners had sold their house and were going to take Sassy to the pound to be put to sleep. I couldn't let that happen, so I took her and kept her in the shed in our backyard, where she slept on the ground next to my bike. My dad didn't like animals, so Sassy was my secret.

She followed me everywhere except her old house. When I turned to ride down that part of the street, she'd sit and wait, almost a quarter mile away, for me to return. Even after the people moved and the house was empty she still wouldn't go down that street.

One day, when I got home, I discovered the secret was out.

"What's that dog doing out in the shed?" asked my dad.

I told him the truth. To my surprise, he let me keep her.

Still, I didn't trust him. A couple of weeks later, I went out to the shed, and Sassy wasn't there. I thought Dad must have taken her to the pound. I ran inside.

"Where's my dog?" I asked Mom.

"Billy, have you seen the dog?" Mom asked Dad.

He just shook his head.

Two days went by, then three, then four, then five, and there was still no sign of Sassy. I couldn't believe she'd run away. I was sure Dad had gotten rid of her.

On Saturday morning, I heard my dad calling me. I pulled on my clothes and ran outside.

"Come here," said my dad. He was pointing to the small trap door next to the fuel tank that led under the house. It was slightly ajar.

"Look inside," said my dad.

I got down on my hands and knees and pulled the little door completely open. I saw Sassy under the house.

"Sassy, Sassy, Sassy!" I yelled, and crawled all the way inside.

She wasn't alone: she had puppies, five of them.

Dad gave me one of his old drop cloths, and I fluffed it up and made a nest for Sassy in the shed. Dad carried the pups over there, and Sassy followed.

"Which one do you like best?" asked Dad.

Three of them were black, like Sassy. One was black with some white patches, and the smallest was black and white in the same amounts all over.

"This one," I said, picking him up. He was just a little ball of fuzz, so I named him Fuzzy.

Before long, the pups grew bigger and started wandering around the yard. They started needing regular food. I cared about them, but I was too young to look after them properly, and the responsibility fell on Mom. This extra chore was the last thing she needed.

Still, I was upset when I got back from school one day to find my dad had given them away—all except Fuzzy.

"They were getting too big and needed a home," Mom explained.

I didn't believe her. I knew dad had taken them to the pound. I never said a word to him about it, but I hated him for not telling me before he took them, so I could say good-bye. Plus, much as I loved Fuzzy, if I'd had the choice, I'd rather have kept Sassy. I felt like crying, but for the first time, no tears came.

Fortunately for me Fuzzy was almost a carbon copy of his mother. He was smart, loyal, affectionate, and followed me everywhere. Even as a puppy, he'd guard my bike, growling if anybody came near it. He was a true friend.

•

I soon got tired of delivering papers, so I quit. I kept it to myself, though I knew it was just a matter of time before my father found out. I continued to go for long bike rides, sometimes as far as the Key Bridge, twenty miles away.

One night, I was late getting home. It had started to grow

dark, and my bike light batteries were dead. I knew my parents would be getting worried about me, but Fuzzy had been following me all day and was getting tired. I had to stop and let him rest. When I finally got home, I rode through the neighbor's backyard, left my bike in the shed and walked to the kitchen door. I could already feel the tension and hostility inside.

Mom was standing by the sink; Dad was on the other side of the room, in the doorway. I recognized the expression on my mother's face—pure fear. I used to think she somehow instigated Dad's violence, but by this time I'd come to realize this wasn't the case. Whatever the source of his rage, it was purely internal.

"Go and wash, and I'll heat up your dinner," said Mom. She was in the submissive mood that I'd come to connect with Dad's abuse. It was the way she acted after he'd hit her. The mood in the room frightened me. I just stood there staring down at the stains on the floor.

"You're supposed to be home before dark," said Dad, sharply. "Where've you been?"

"I was looking for new customers."

"Go to your room. You can forget about your dinner. I ought to beat your ass."

As soon as I closed my bedroom door, the yelling and arguing started up. I got into bed, but I couldn't sleep. Finally, I heard Mom and Dad going to bed as well. Then I started to hear sounds coming from their room. I'd heard these sounds before. Mom would make moaning noises and beg, "No, please, Billy, no." It sounded as though Dad was hurting her. Later, I discovered he was a sexual sadist who enjoyed verbally and physically abusing my mother, breaking her down emotionally, and then forcing her to have sex with him in degrading and painful ways.

The next morning, I realized that sometime during the night, I'd pissed in the bed. Confused and embarrassed, I got dressed and, leaving the bed unmade, went into the kitchen. Mom had fixed Cream of Wheat, my favorite breakfast. While I was eating, she went to the bedroom, emerging a few minutes later with my dirty sheets, which she put in the washing machine. To my relief, she never said a word about the stains.

That day, I skipped school and rode my bike to the new shopping center at Seven Corners, about fifteen miles away. I could easily get there and back before dark. By 11 a.m, with Fuzzy running by my side, I'd made it as far as the bowling alley at Falls Church. Normally, it was full of life—music coming from the juke box, young guys hanging out, talking and laughing, the sound of balls rolling down the chutes, people cheering when the pins were knocked down—so I was surprised to find a sign on the door that said: "Closed for repairs." A recent snowfall had caused the roof to cave in. Sorely disappointed, I rode on to Seven Corners, home of the biggest shopping center I'd ever seen. Leaving Fuzzy to guard my bike at an isolated side entrance, I wandered through every store in the mall, which had two levels. By the time I'd finished exploring, I was tired and hungry. It was time to head home.

When I got back, Mom looked worried. "Your Dad called

from the firehouse," she said. "He wants you to stay in your room until he gets home. What did you do?"

"I don't know," I said, starting to wonder what it could be. Had someone told him I'd quit my paper route? What about skipping school—did he know about that? Maybe someone had recognized me that afternoon at Seven Corners, and decided to give him a call. The fact is, I'd broken any number of rules.

I didn't feel like sticking around to get another ass whipping, so I decided to get out of there as soon as I could. I broke open my brown glass piggy bank and pocketed four dollars in change. Next, I changed into clean clothes and put on my heavy coat. I had no particular plans, but I knew it was getting dark and starting to snow.

"Where are you going?" asked Mom.

I told her the truth, "I don't know."

Leaving behind Fuzzy and my bike, I headed for the rail-road tracks, about a mile down Cedar Lane. The snow was coming down fast, and I could feel the cold even through my heavy coat. If I kept walking down the tracks, I'd be in Vienna in about half an hour; after that, I had no idea what would happen, or where I'd spend the night. I tried not to think about it.

Where the railroad tracks crossed Route 123, I stopped to light my last cigarette. It was a Winston—Mom had changed brands. I broke off the filter, struck the match, and inhaled. I'd finally learned to smoke without coughing—a small achievement, maybe, but I felt a little more like a man.

When I got to Vienna, I went into a Laundromat to rest for

a while and get warm, but the people washing their clothes seemed to be looking at me suspiciously, so I decided to press on. My last experience of running away from home had left me feeling paranoid, and this time I was determined to trust nobody except myself. I set off walking to Tyson's Corner, where the road intersected with Route 7. I figured if I could catch a ride, I'd head for D.C., but a lot of cars passed by before a trucker took pity on me and pulled over.

"Where you headed?"

"Key Bridge."

"Well, I can take you as far as Route 7."

"Thanks, Mister."

The trucker was heading to a small town called Leesburg, and it was so warm in his cab that for a while I thought about changing my mind and going there with him, but I decided it would be hard for me to keep a low profile in such a small town. All too soon, we got to the intersection of Route 123 and Route 7. The snow was still coming down like crazy, and there was over an inch on the ground.

"Thanks for the ride, Mister," I said, climbing out. Sorry to leave the warmth of the truck, I walked over to the first place I saw and went inside.

"You can't come in here, boy", someone said. "This is a beer joint."

The only other place in sight was a country store across the street, which was obviously closed.

As I stood there feeling cold and desperate, a car pulled into the lot in front of the beer joint. The driver got out and went inside, leaving the motor running. I could see the exhaust fumes exhaust blowing out of the tail pipe into the snow. Without even thinking about it, I ran to the car and got in the driver's side. The seat was still warm. I'd learned a lot about cars from hanging out in the junkyard, climbing around in the shells of old wrecks. I'd driven plenty of Go-Carts and Bumper Cars, and I figured I could easily handle a three-speed stick shift. I was wrong.

I released the handbrake, pulled down on the gearshift, put my foot on the gas pedal and released the clutch. The car suddenly jerked forward then started jumping toward the highway, its wheels spinning in the snow. I got to the road, grinding and bolting, but everything was out of control. I couldn't manage to shift gears or control the car's direction in the snow. I couldn't even see which side of the road I was on. I managed to bounce the car a half-mile or so down Route 7, out of the sight of the beer joint, but when I tried to change gear, it bolted forward again, and I slammed on the brakes without pushing in the clutch. The car jerked to a complete stop, the engine cut out, then I felt it sliding onto the hard shoulder. I turned the keys again, but nothing happened.

At that point, I should have jumped out and started running, but it was warm in the car, and I sat there for a moment or two, trying to figure out what to do next. Suddenly, I saw flashing red lights behind me. Then a cop was standing there with a gun in one hand and a flashlight in the other. When he saw I was just a kid, he put away his gun, got out his handcuffs, and put me in the back seat of his car. Pretty soon, I was on my way the Juvenile Detention Center.

I was in a room by myself when my Dad came in, looking angrier than I'd ever seen him. At the sight of his face, my whole body started shaking. Fortunately, they kept me overnight, so I didn't have to face a beating right then. The next day, I found myself standing before a judge, who charged me with "unauthorized use of a motor vehicle." My guilt was obvious, but nobody asked the simple question: why?

•

"GET UP, LET'S GO."

"Where?"

"Just follow me kid, you'll find out soon enough."

He was a short, stocky man: a big round head, a flat top haircut, brown pants, white shirt, black shoes. He wasn't a cop, so I figured he had to be a detention worker.

I followed him down the hall. We walked so quickly I didn't get the chance to look at anything. All I saw were rows of doors with a small vertical window in each. We passed at least ten of these on both sides before reaching the end of the hall. The door in front of us was locked, but the man was carrying a key ring that contained at least fifty keys. He opened the door, leading me into another hallway. I kept looking for a way to escape.

Finally, the man stopped, opened a door and turned on a light. The room was windowless. It contained a shower stall and a long table piled with stacks of folded laundry, each with a small brown paper bag on top.

"Here," he said, handing me one of the piles. There was a

towel, washcloth, a pair of blue jeans with no pockets and an elastic waist, a long sleeved blue shirt with snaps instead of buttons, and a pair of white socks. In the brown bag was a small tube of toothpaste, a bar of soap, and a toothbrush.

"Take a shower, get dressed. Put your clothes and shoes on the table. Keep your own underwear."

I didn't want to take a shower, but his tone of voice made me nervous. I had no desire to find out what would happen if I refused, so I got undressed and put my clothes on the table. The floor was icy cold. I showered quickly and got dressed. The clothes he'd given me were all much too big. As soon as I pulled my own pants, the man came back through the door.

I reached for my shoes.

"No shoes," he said. "Come with me."

We walked back through the hallway side-by-side.

"First door on the right," he said.

I turned the knob, but it was locked. He opened the door with his keys and switched on the light. The dim, window-less room contained a small bed, a toilet, and a sink. On the bed were sheets and an army blanket. There was no pillow.

"Don't I get toilet paper?"

"No shit paper on this shift. Keep your cheeks shut till to-morrow morning." With that, he left me alone in the room, locking the door behind him.

It was official. At eleven years old, I'd been arrested, charged, and placed in the custody of the Fairfax County Police Department. This is how it all began.

I looked through the narrow window in my door. I could

see into the room across from mine; it was empty. I peered up and down the halls; there was no one in sight. It was creepy quiet. I was too young to make sense of what was happening to me, too inexperienced to understand the seriousness of what I'd done. Under the circumstances, I felt justified in stealing the car. It had seemed like the only alternative. I couldn't understand why I was being punished for it.

Keeping my clothes on, I lay down on the mattress, using the sheets and blanket for a pillow. I couldn't switch off the light—the controls were in the hallway—so I wrapped the towel round my head to cover my eyes and fell asleep quickly. Sometime during the night, the light was turned off.

I woke early in the morning, when it was still dark. There was a little light coming from the window in the door, and when my eyes had adjusted to the darkness, I got up and looked out of the window again. There was still no one in sight, but then I heard a toilet flush in the distance, assuring me I wasn't completely alone. I fell asleep again, and a couple of hours later the lights came on.

"Get ready for breakfast!" someone yelled.

A few minutes passed, then the door opened.

"Follow me," I was told.

One by one, six of us—four boys and two girls, all older than me—were escorted into a large room containing six tables, a television set, a Ping-Pong table, and a couple of lounge chairs. There were also some adjoining rooms; these, I later learned, were used for group meetings and police interviews. The room had bay windows overlooking the recreation yard. I joined the end of the breakfast line, taking one of the trays that were passed through a slot in the kitchen wall. I sat alone at a table. My tray contained a small metal bowl of dry cereal, a carton of milk, a fried egg, a couple of pieces of bread and some applesauce. I made an egg-and-applesauce sandwich, drank the milk, and left the cereal. One by one, as we each finished our breakfast, we took our trays back to the slot in the wall and were escorted to our rooms.

Less than a half hour later, a man came to my door—not the short man, but a man I hadn't seen before. He handed me my clothes and shoes and told me I was going out to court.

I rode to the courthouse in the back seat of a white state car. There were no handles to open the car doors and no knobs to roll down the windows, so there was no way I could escape. Eventually, we arrived at a small building between the courthouse and the city jail. On the side of the building, it said "Juvenile Domestic Relations Court." For some reason, I felt disappointed that it wasn't a big courtroom like the one on *Perry Mason*. It was just an ordinary room with everyday tables and chairs, no Judge's bench, no court reporters, no gallery.

My mom and dad were waiting for me, and we were allowed to visit for a few minutes before the Judge came in. My dad said nothing, and I didn't look at him. Mom looked sad. She tried to reach out to me, but I turned away. I was frightened and angry.

The informal hearing lasted for about twenty minutes. Since everybody was dressed in ordinary clothes, I didn't know which person was the Judge was until he spoke.

"Son, can you tell me why you tried to steal this man's car?"

He was waiting for me to speak, but I said nothing. I could see they were only interested in why I stole the car, not why I'd run away from home.

"Answer the judge," demanded my dad. "He's asking you a question."

I was reminded, then, of how threatening my father could be, and I knew I didn't want to go back home with him. I couldn't take another of his beatings.

"Because I wanted to," I said, "and I'd do it again."

After that, there was no chance of me being sent back home with my parents.

"Young man," said the judge, "you appear to be incorrigible. You could have killed someone, or hurt yourself, trying to drive that car. By your own admission, you stole it, and you might well steal another. There's no question about your guilt. However, I do have questions concerning proper disposition in sentencing. I'm ordering the Commonwealth's attorney to investigate your school records and attendance, speak with your parents, and make recommendations to this Court. You'll appear here again in two weeks from this date. At that time, I'll render my decision. Until then, you'll remain in the custody of the Northern Virginia Juvenile Detention Center."

My mom looked shocked when they took me away. I didn't look at my father. The only thing that stuck with me was the word "incorrigible." What did it mean?

On the way back, I had mixed emotions. While I didn't want to go back to the Detention Center, I certainly didn't want to be sent back to my dad.

I stayed at the center for the next two weeks, and soon got bored and restless. Every morning at 6 a.m., they got us up and took us to breakfast in the multipurpose room, then took us back to our rooms until 10:30, when we were allowed out for indoor recreation: television, board games, and Ping-Pong. There was no outside recreation, since it was winter. They kept trying to get me to join the group activities, but I'd never participate. I couldn't sit still long enough for board games. Ping-Pong was the only thing I liked, and I got pretty good at it. Once I played one of the staff members, and he cheated. This made me so mad that I punched out a window, breaking the right knuckle of my little finger. They had to take me out to hospital to get my hand put in a cast. When I got back, they put me in "quiet time" for the rest of the day, which was their usual form of punishment. Whenever anybody acted out, they were placed in their room for "quiet time."

After that, during indoor recreation, I'd just walk round the room, stopping by the bay windows to look out over the recreation yard. One day, one of the girls tried to talk to me. Her name was Corina. She was older than me, and I was too shy to say anything. I met her again a few years later, when things were different.

Time passed quickly. People came from the Court to talk with me, but I didn't trust them, and I refused to cooperate. Then my mom came to visit me.

"You'll be going to see the judge again tomorrow," she said.

"Where's dad?"

"Outside in the car. We can't be there tomorrow, but don't worry, you'll soon be home."

I didn't see her again for over two months.

•

THE HEARING LASTED less than ten minutes. I stood on one side of a long table with my escort, while the Judge and a young woman spoke to one another on the other side. I had no idea what would happen to me, and I was so nervous I was squirming in my shoes. The woman made notes as the Judge spoke. My escort stood erect with his arms and hands folded at his belt buckle. The walls were hung with pictures of old men in suits and robes, and framed documents. In the corners, there were flags on wooden poles. I was looking out of the window when I heard the word, "Beaumont." I realized the Judge was addressing me. I turned to look at him. Now that he knew he had my attention, he repeated what he'd just said from the beginning, speaking slowly and clearly.

"It's my decision," he said, "that you're to be placed in the custody of the Beaumont School for Boys, in Beaumont, Virginia, for a period of no longer than six months. It's my intention that you'll carefully reflect on the attitude and behavior that brought you to this court, and that you'll learn to respect and accept the guidance from your parents and others in authority upon your return."

I said nothing.

"Do you have any questions?"

Shaking my head, I wondered how long six months was.

He made it sound like a hundred years. The Judge stood up, and my escort took my arm and walked me to the car. We drove back to the Detention Center in silence. I gazed out of the window, looking at people, cars, buildings, everything I was no longer a part of. Now, I was on my own.

Back at the Detention Center, people soon learned they were sending me to Beaumont. I didn't know where Beaumont was, or what it was like, but it seemed to make me some kind of celebrity. Everyone wanted to talk to me.

"What happened?" asked Corina. "What did they say?"

"They're sending me to Beaumont for six months, so I can think about what I did."

"When are you leaving?"

"I don't know."

I wanted to seem tough, as though I didn't care. It was true that I didn't really care where they sent me, but I definitely wasn't tough. If anything, I'd been weakened by my father's beatings. His constant abuse had taken its toll, leaving me scared and helpless. I had very little sense of my own identity, and no impulse for self-preservation, let alone self-respect. What other people saw as criminal behavior was just me thrashing around like a wounded animal, in pain and out of control.

I walked over to the bay windows, and Corina followed me. We stood there for several minutes without saying a word. It was an uncomfortable feeling. I wanted to talk to her, but my mind was blank.

"Boy!" someone called. I turned around. It was the man with the flattop haircut. He led me back to my room, where

I was instructed to remove my own clothes and put my uniform back on. I got changed then started to go back to the multi-purpose room to see Corinna, but the man stopped me.

"We've got to keep you segregated," he said.

"What do you mean, segregated?"

"It's policy. You need to be apart from the other children. They'll be coming for you in a couple of days, and we need you to stay in your room."

"A couple of *days*? Why?"

"It's policy," he said. "You can go to the rec room for half an hour at meal times. If you want to shower, you can do it at night."

For the next two days, I didn't see any of the other kids except when they came out for meals and rec room. I would wait at my door for them, peering through the window. When I wasn't there, Corina would tap on the glass.

They took me to Beaumont in January 1959, in a brand-new, black, four-door Ford with no door or window knobs in the back seat. We pulled out right after lunch, when Corina and the others were locked up, so none of them saw me leave. It didn't really matter. I was anxious to get away.

We were in the car for a long time. At first, I looked out of the window, trying to identify the make, model, and year of all the vehicles we passed on the highway. We overtook a lot of cars, and this made me curious about the driver, and why he was going so fast. From what I could see of him, he was short and thin, an old guy, at least sixty. Later, I learned he was in charge of security at Beaumont, which meant he'd be the one coming after me if I tried to run away. They said he had a nose like a bloodhound and could outrun a rabbit. I believed it, at least for a while.

Eventually I must have fallen asleep; the next thing I knew, the driver was telling me we were about a mile away from Beaumont.

"Time to wake up, boy," he said. "Look over there. That's the women's prison. We're getting ready to cross the James River."

I had butterflies in my stomach, knowing we were almost there. We drove across the bridge then turned right on Beaumont Road, which took us up a hill. On the left were big houses, then a small white church; on the right was open land. We drove past a few more buildings, and I saw the campus surrounding a large playing field. We pulled up outside the infirmary, which is where I spent the night.

When I arrived there in 1959, Beaumont was nothing but a large farm on thousand or so acres of land. Apart from the crops and animals, there was a school, a gym, a chow hall, a barber's shop and a place for fixing cars, as well as a church, infirmary, and the four cottages where we lived. When we weren't in school or in the auto shop, we were expected to work, and hard. That was something I soon learned all about.

My first morning at Beaumont they brought me breakfast in bed. After breakfast, they told me I'd need medical clearance before they could assign me to a cottage, so I was taken to see the doctor, an unremarkable middle-aged man who asked me a lot of questions and didn't really seem interested in my answers.

Suddenly, he stood up and pulled a curtained partition in front of us.

"Drop your pants," he said.

Reluctantly, I pulled my pants down to my knees.

"Alright, let's have a look. I need to see if you've got any VD. Have you been sexually active?"

"Yes," I lied.

"You're uncircumcised," he said. "I need you to pull the skin back over your penis."

I did as he said. I knew "penis" was a word people some used to mean dick.

"Alright," he said. "We're all done. Go and tell the nurse you're cleared."

I pulled up my pants and went to find the nurse. I was glad to hear I was cleared, even though I didn't know what it meant. I didn't know what "VD" meant, either, or "uncircumcised." I just knew they sounded bad, like "incorrigible."

The infirmary door opened and someone came to take me to my cottage. It was the old guy who'd driven me here the day before.

"Come on, boy," he said. "You're going to B Cottage."

I followed him across the playing field, through a big yard in front of the chow hall, to a large, two-story house with a long, dormitory-style wing built onto the sides. We went down a flight of steps, through a basement door and up to a large wooden desk where a guy was sitting reading a newspaper.

"Hey, Nelly," said the old man. "I brought you some new fish to fry."

"Okay," said the guy behind the desk. He looked up from the paper and I noticed his left eye was made of glass. This man's name was Mr. Nelson. Behind his back, I heard the boys called him either Nelly or Dead Eye. He was the "Father" of B Cottage—and, I later learned, the most strict and abusive of all Cottage "Fathers."

The old man left. I expected Nelly to give me a big sermon or a list of rules, but he just ignored me, going back to his newspaper.

I looked around. To my left was a wall of lockers. In two corners of the room there were single chairs facing the wall. Two boys were sitting in these chairs. In the middle of the room there were five wooden benches, the kind you see in church, and above the benches was a television on a shelf hanging from the ceiling. I later learned each bench would hold four or five guys, depending on the size of their ass, and the first two benches were always reserved for certain boys. I would never be among them.

•

B COTTAGE WAS DESIGNATED for boys between the ages of twelve to fifteen, and I was just about to turn twelve. There were around twenty-five of us. I picked out a locker and sat down in the last row of benches in front of the television. I was afraid to speak to anyone. Dead Eye was still sitting reading his paper. Next to his desk was an open doorway leading to the latrine. This was a big bathroom containing three urinals and four toilets separated by metal partitions, which provided some privacy. In the middle of the room was a large round washbasin with a spigot. Across the back wall were five showerheads. These showers, as I soon learned, were the venue for a lot of devious behavior, pranks, and the occasional fight.

A few older boys were playing cards at a table. I listened in on their conversation while pretending to watch TV. I was afraid they were talking about me, but to my surprise, they didn't seem interested. No one was paying me any attention; it was as though I didn't exist. That would change soon enough.

On the second day, while marching in a single file to the chow hall, the boy behind me kicked my foot, making me trip. I caught my balance and looked at him.

"What are you doing?"

The boy said nothing, and gave a dark smile.

A few seconds later, we stopped in front of the chow hall. Mr. Nelson went to the side of the front entrance, picked up a straw broom that was leaning against the wall, broke off the handle and started walking over.

"Boy," he called.

"Yes sir," I responded in terror.

"Step out of line," he barked.

Everyone was quiet and still, waiting. They knew what was coming next.

"Put out your right hand," he ordered.

As I did so, he grabbed my wrist and whacked my knuckles with a swift, hard downward blow. The pain shot up my arm and I yelled out loud. Mr. Nelson pulled my wrist in a turning motion so my backside faced him. In the same flowing movement, he swung the broom handle as hard as he could across the back of my thighs.

I cried out in pain. My legs gave out under me, and I fell to the ground.

"Get up," he said. "The first one was for talking, the second one was for stepping out of line. When we get back, you're in the corner chair for an hour."

No one had told me anything about the rules or routines, so I didn't know what was forbidden. I never talked in line again, but that wasn't the last time I got a beating. In fact, I got another one the next day. They made us walk in single file to the gym for recreation. The same kid was behind me, and he tried to trip me again. I was so angry I lost control of myself and took a swing, hitting the side of his head. He grabbed me and we both fell on the ground wrestling.

"Stop!" yelled Dead Eye.

Everyone stopped. Mr. Nelson pulled us out of line, seated everyone else in the bleachers, and led me and the other kid to the back of the gym. From a closet, he took two pairs of enormous boxing gloves, about as big as my head.

"Looks like you two want to fight. Put on the gloves. You're going to box each other until I tell you to stop. Understand?"

"Yes sir."

"And if you stop before I tell you," he added, pulling off his belt, folding it in half and slapping it gently against his hand, "I'm going to beat your ass with this belt until you start boxing again. So, you have a choice, fight each other or take a worse whipping from me."

We stood there, staring at him.

"So? What are you waiting for? Start swinging!"

Suddenly, something smacked me on the side of the head and knocked me to the floor.

"Get up!" yelled Dead Eye.

We swung at each other, but it was impossible—it felt like we were having a pillow fight, only with hard pillows. Although the gloves were made of soft padded leather, they hurt like hell. My face was getting red and scratched all over; it felt like I was badly sunburned. My nose felt as if it was broken. We quickly got too tired to swing, and were soon fighting in slow motion. Dead Eye made us go on for another fifteen minutes, until we were both crying, and could hardly stand.

"Do you still want to fight?" he asked.

We both shook our heads.

Dead Eye made us both spend the night in the corner chairs in B Cottage, staring at the wall. His punishment was terrible, but it worked—it stopped me from wanting to fight anybody for a very long time.

Dead Eye might have been the worst of them all, but he was far from the only threatening adult at Beaumont. There was a night watchman who patrolled the grounds at night. In the summer time, when the windows were open, he'd occasionally sneak up and catch guys talking, or out of their beds. If he caught someone after lights out, doing something besides using the toilet, the night watchman would put you on punishment, which meant you had to stand at attention at the end of your bed. I don't know how, but I never got caught or punished by the night watchman.

On weekends, where there was no school or shop, Mr. Nelson got additional staff to help supervise the cottage, and Mrs. Nelson, who we seldom saw, washed our clothes. On my first weekend, Mr. Nelson called for me. He was upstairs in his makeshift office. I walked up the steps from the basement to the first floor.

"Come in here and sit down, boy," he said. "Is this your first time in trouble?"

"Yes."

"Do your mother and father still live together?"

"Yes."

"Are you an only child?"

"No. I have a brother." I didn't know it at the time, but my mom was pregnant again.

Mr. Nelson had a file on the desk in front of him.

"Has your father ever been arrested?" he asked.

"I don't think so. I don't know."

At that moment, his wife called him from downstairs.

"Just stay here," he said. "I'll be right back."

While he was gone, I sneaked a quick look at the file on the desk. The top sheet was an arrest report in my father's name. According to the report, he'd been arrested a number of times: driving on a suspended permit, shoplifting, drunk and disorderly, and, at the bottom of the page, a single word: Rape.

I went back to my seat.

When Mr. Nelson came back, he told me I'd be starting school on Monday morning and I'd be working in a farm detail in the afternoon, and whenever there was no school. He also told me I wasn't allowed visits for sixty days.

I soon got to know the routine. Every weekday, at 8 a.m. and again at 1 p.m., boys from all the cottages would line up in single file at a designated area. There, the old man who could run faster than a rabbit would call out school, shop, and work assignments for the day. When your assignment was called, you'd fall out of line and go to wherever they sent you. At the end of the class or assignment, you'd report back to your cottage.

On Monday, they sent me to school. I had to take tests so they could find my grade level. I didn't pay much attention to the tests. I'd never had any interest in school, and this time was no different. Instead of focusing on the tests, I thought about the fact that my dad had been arrested for rape. I suddenly realized why Aunt Peggy didn't want to leave me on my own with my cousin Laura. She must have assumed the impulse was hereditary. Maybe it was.

●

THAT AFTERNOON, I listened as the assignments were called out. They put me on farm work detail with around twenty boys, including two others from B cottage. We marched to the big barn, home to a bunch of smelly hogs that would eat almost anything. Our jobs included feeding and cleaning up after the animals, harvesting the crops, loading and unloading trucks and trailers, cutting the grass, picking up the trash, and lots of other tasks.

I was still not yet twelve, which meant I was always the youngest in any group or activity. I'd learned to keep my mouth shut and not to draw attention to myself; still, there was never a day that went by that someone didn't try to bully, abuse, or humiliate me. In most ways, I didn't measure up compared to the other boys. I felt so inadequate that I tried to work harder than all the others on the farm. Although this sometimes got me praise and attention from the staff, it would often get me in trouble with the other boys, who'd be expected to keep up with me.

There were times and places where I was particularly scared and vulnerable. For example, after each farm work detail I'd have to take a shower with the other boys. At the Detention Center, I hadn't had to use the bathroom or take a shower in front of anyone, and I tried not to let the other boys see how terrified I was to be naked in front of them. I was painfully shy, inhibited and self-conscious about my body. At Beaumont, a boy's masculinity was measured by how much facial hair he had, how much hair on his arms and legs, and especially how much pubic hair. Boys with big muscular arms were also regarded as tough. Unfortunately, I failed in every area of masculinity. I had no facial hair, no pubic hair, and only peach fuzz on my arms and legs. I was slim, and my arms were small. I didn't measure up.

Most days, in the shower, someone would start a pissing contest. The winner would be the boy who'd been able to hold the most liquid in his bladder all day. I tried to avoid getting involved, but I'd often get caught in the middle, or end up as the target. Even if I'd wanted to join in, I wouldn't have been able to pull the trigger. I was used to being in the bathroom alone and locking the door, and I was so inhibited it was almost impossible for me to piss if someone was watching me. It would be several years before I could even piss with another person in the room.

One hot day, we were working in the fields overlooking James River and the Women's Penitentiary.

"Hey, if you listen," someone said, "you can hear the women yelling at you from inside the prison."

"If those women could get a hold of one of you boys, they'd eat you up. You wouldn't make it out of there alive," said the staff supervisor, looking straight at me. Everybody laughed. I tried to imagine what he meant. What would they do to me? I didn't understand.

When we got back to the cottage, we went to shower in groups of five. I was in the second group. While we were waiting to get in, I noticed one of the older boys looking at me and smiling. This kid, Stoney, had nicknames for all of us. He called me "little queer."

"Come on little queer, get your ass in here," he said.

As soon as I stepped into the shower, he hit me with a stream of yellow piss from his dick. I jumped out of the way, slipped, and fell on my ass. Everyone burst out laughing.

"You boys cut out the horse play, or there won't be any TV tonight," yelled Dead Eye. That day I got off easy. Most of the time it didn't work out that way.

Stone called me "little queer" for a reason. My first group shower made me aware of something I hadn't been conscious of before—that I was uncircumcised, though at the time I'd never heard the word. I just noticed that there was something different about my dick. Some guys called them pricks, some called them peckers, some said cocks, and some said dicks. I wondered if my kind had a special name. There were twenty or twenty-five boys in our cottage, and I was determined to check them all out to see if any of them had a dick like mine. Dead Eye would only let five boys get in the shower at a time; when one came out, another took his place. I stayed in the shower longer each day, waiting to check out everyone's dick. When guys caught me looking, some would be embarrassed and turn away; others would get angry and threaten me; a couple even punched me, but I didn't stop looking. Some guys' dicks were bigger or longer than others, but apart from size they were all pretty much the same. No one had a dick like mine.

Before I got to Beaumont, I knew nothing about homosexuality. I learned fast. One day, during class, I said I needed to use the bathroom. I didn't really need to go; I just wanted to get out of the class for a few minutes. The school bathroom was like a gas station bathroom. You had to take a key attached to a piece of wood from a hook by the door, and walk around the side of the building. I took the key, left the classroom, went around the corner, and saw that the bathroom door was open. I walked through the door, and, in the corner, I saw a boy standing in front of another boy who was sitting on the toilet. When I walked in, the boy standing got scared and backed up, and I realized his dick had been in the other guy's mouth. We all froze for a moment, terrified, then the standing boy yelled, "Get your ass outta here!"

Without a word, I turned and went back to class.

For a long time, I thought about what I saw. I couldn't get it out of my head. I never told anyone. Neither of the boys was in my class, or my cottage. I couldn't imagine what they'd been doing. I'd seen boys going into the dorm bathroom and staying there a long time; I'd walked into the latrine and caught boys playing with themselves, and I'd noticed their dicks would be hard, but I knew nothing about masturbation. I'd recently turned twelve, and I was still extremely naïve about anything to do with sex.

On Saturday morning, Mr. Nelson called me to the stairway in the rec room.

"Boy, your mother called," he said. "Your folks are paying you a visit. They should be here sometime this afternoon, so you'd better clean yourself up."

I hadn't seen my mom and dad for over two months. Away from them, I'd forgotten what things had been like at home. I started to look forward to the visit.

It was a nice day, sunny, but cold. My folks arrived around 2:00 pm. We could either spend our visit indoors, or sit outside on the front lawn. We decided to try and bear the cold, and we sat at the picnic tables in front of B cottage. The visit lasted no more than a half hour, though later, during warmer weather, they came for longer visits, and mom would bring a picnic lunch. Dad was full of questions about the farm, and the kind of work I was doing.

"What do they feed you? How's the food?" Mom kept asking.

I wanted to know how Fuzzy was doing.

"He stays around the house a lot since you've been gone," she said.

It felt good to see Mom and Dad. I didn't feel bad when they left, but I wouldn't have minded going with them.

Mom brought me some treats: candy bars, cookies, chewing gum, a deck of playing cards, and a board game that I never played. Dead Eye looked through the bag, then gave it back to me.

"Put it in your locker," he said.

I didn't listen. Over the next couple of days, I gave it all away. Guys would ask me for stuff, and I couldn't say no. I guess I was a sucker.

One afternoon, our work crew was sent to the chow hall to help unload trucks in the downstairs storeroom. The lady in charge of this storeroom was missing three of her fingers on her right hand. No one knew how she lost her fingers, but there was a rumor that if you were ever alone with her, she'd give you a two-finger hand job. I wasn't exactly sure what that meant, but I figured it meant she would play with your dick.

When we got to the storeroom, the lady came outside to the trailers where we were working, and I took a look at her right hand. It only had a thumb and a pinky finger. It looked weird. She picked me and two other boys to come inside to help her. The others were left to unload and stack boxes of canned food, sugar and dried milk.

The three of us followed her inside, to the big walk-in freezer. She showed us where she wanted to put the stuff then she took us to the next room, where there were crates of eggs, milk, and vegetables.

"Put everything where I showed you," she said. Then she looked at me, reached out, grabbed my wrist with her two fingers and pulled me toward a door just in front of us. "I need some things up here, so you can come with me."

•

I STOOD MOTIONLESS while she picked through her ring of keys, looking for the one that fit the silver padlock on the door. She was wearing a stiff white cotton dress, with buttons all the way up the front. The top one was undone, exposing part of her bra. Her legs were bare, and she had on the kind of heavy, white shoes that nurses wear. I found myself staring at her until the click of the padlock reminded me where I was.

The door opened a small pantry lined with shelves containing condiments, coffee, tea, and a variety of neatly arranged cooking utensils. There was a ladder leaning against the shelves, and the lady with the missing fingers started to climb it.

"Hold the bottom of this ladder, and don't let me fall," she instructed.

I moved behind her, so that her ass was directly in my face. As she climbed the ladder, I thought about squatting down and trying to look up her dress, but I was too nervous. I was close enough to smell her. I'd once overheard some older boys talking about how a girl's pussy smells like fish, but I couldn't smell anything at all.

Holding the ladder, I couldn't help brushing my arm

against the skin of her calves, and as I touched her, I felt something rising in my pants. I wanted to run my hand up her dress and explore between her legs, but I didn't dare. The feeling was scary and strange.

As the lady began stepping backwards down the ladder, I let go and just stood there awkwardly, blocking the doorway. She was a few inches taller than me, and when she turned around her breasts were right in my face. The only time I'd seen a woman's breasts was when I saw my aunt feeding her baby. I felt as though I wanted to say or do something, but I didn't know what it was.

"Come on boy, let's go," she said, brushing past me. She sounded angry. Did I do something wrong? I wondered if she'd been expecting me to touch her or do something to her. Maybe she was annoyed when I didn't. Maybe she thought I wasn't good enough.

"Alright!" she yelled, locking the door. "Everybody back outside! Back to the trailer!"

None of the other boys ever asked me what happened while I was alone with the lady with the missing fingers. If they had, I would have lied and made something up.

The days passed slowly at Beaumont. If you kept track of time, everything seemed to slow down. After four months, I started to think about running away. At home, I knew where I was; here, I was afraid I'd get lost in the woods with no food or water. If Beaumont had been anywhere near a city, I'd have tried to escape, but it was smack in the middle of nowhere.

One Sunday afternoon in the early spring of 1959, I had

a visit from Mom and Dad. The neatly cut lawn out in front of B Cottage was full of families sitting at picnic tables with their boys. It reminded me of hanging out at the beach, only there was no sand and no water. Mom was heavily pregnant, but she didn't say anything about the baby, and she didn't mention my little brother Buddy. She'd brought my favorite foods: fried chicken, coleslaw, potato salad, and watermelon. She told me how Fuzzy was doing and chatted about people in our neighborhood and the weather, but after that it felt like no one had anything to say. No one said, "We miss you," or "We love you," or "We can't wait for you to come home." In fact, Dad said almost nothing. He just lay back in the recliner chair he'd brought with him. I could tell he'd been drinking. When they left, Dad said, "Stay out of trouble," and Mom said, "Are you sure you don't want to take a piece of this chicken with you?" There were no hugs or handshakes, just a wave good bye as they drove away. The only positive thing about the visit was Dad's new car. It was a black 1958 Chevy Impala with white wall tires—a popular model at the time. It felt great when some of the boys commented on it. "Your dad's got a neat car," they said. It wasn't much, but it made me feel better, and I needed all the positive recognition I could get.

I'd been sent to Beaumont for six months. The last two months went by pretty fast. There was a tradition that, when someone was getting close to his release date, Dead Eye would announce how many more days he had to go. When somebody was leaving, the other boys would take the opportunity to make their lives as miserable as possible.

"Boy, we've got fifteen days until we get rid of your ass," said Dead Eye one morning. The next day, at daily announcements, it was, "Boy, we've got fourteen days until we get rid of your ass." It should have been a good start to my day, but it was the opposite. In the chow hall, boys would steal food off my tray, mostly milk, cake, pie and fruit. Stoney would come over and put his finger in his nose or down his pants, and then stick it in my mashed potatoes. The last two weeks at Beaumont, I ate very little.

Things got worse. There were no rules or limits to how far the pranks would go. None! Whenever I got in the shower, boys would try to try to stick their fingers up my butt. I didn't get into fights anymore, so guys were always punching me in the arms and chest. They knew I wouldn't retaliate. The day Dead Eye announced I had ten days left, I found a small brown lunch bag on my pillow of my bed. Like a dummy, I opened it. Inside, someone had taken a shit. In the mornings, I would wake up and find myself surrounded by balled-up toilet paper. Stoney had convinced several boys that I was queer, and he'd encouraged them to save the wads of paper when they jerked off, and put them in my bed while I was asleep. Finally, two days before I was supposed to leave, Dead Eye announced that another boy would be going home in two weeks, which took some of the focus off me.

The day before I left, Dead Eye told me, "Boy, I don't think you learned anything while you were here. I'm not sure we should even change your bed sheets. You'll be back."

He was right about that, but he was wrong about me not learning anything. I learned a lot at Beaumont. I learned how to hot-wire cars, how to shoplift, and how to break into soda and candy machines. I learned that some stores and gas stations left money in their cash registers overnight. I learned about breaking into people's houses (you knocked on the front door; if anyone answered you made up a story about having the wrong house; if nobody answered, you went around the back and broke inside). I also learned that some guys liked sucking on each other's dicks, and my dick was different. I was a freak. Finally, I learned I didn't know how to make friends and I couldn't trust anybody, especially not adults.

I left Beaumont on a warm sunny morning, leaving no friends behind. I walked out the front door of B Cottage, down the steps, into my Dad's new '58 Chevy. He'd come to pick me up on his own. When we got home, Mom seemed happy to see me, though Fuzzy barked at me when I got out of the car.

"Fuzzy!" I yelled. His barking stopped, his tail began to wag and he ran over to me. That dog was my only reason to smile.

At Beaumont, I'd wondered many times what I'd do as soon as I got home, and I decided I'd clean my bike. I went over to the shed, and saw the chrome rims on the wheels were beginning to rust.

Mom wanted me to sign up for summer school at Westview Elementary. I think she thought I'd end up in trouble if I didn't have something to do. As it turned out, summer school wasn't so bad. It was all either arts and crafts, or sports and games. I rode there on my bike, and Fuzzy would lie there all day looking after it while I was inside making clay pots and painting in watercolors. In the afternoon we played Ping-Pong, or shot basketball outside.

One day there was a contest to see who could do the most exercise. I was determined to win something. First, we had to do push-ups. I only managed twenty-five, and was soon beaten. Next came chin-ups. I'd never done them before, and found them so hard I could only manage ten. The last contest involved sit-ups, which I'd done at Beaumont. You had to lie down flat, then sit up and touch your toes with your fingers. You had to go on as long as you could. I had no idea how many I needed to do in order win. I did twenty-five, but realized it wasn't enough. I went on and on until I'd done a hundred, when one of the female counselors came over and told me to stop. But I didn't want to stop unless I knew I'd won, and couldn't know I'd won because there were still other boys who were waiting to start. The man who was counting my sit-ups inspired me. "Keep going," he said. "You can do another hundred."

I won the prize for the most sit-ups that day: three hundred and sixty-six. I went home with stomach cramps. The next day, when I woke up, all the muscles in my stomach were sore, and I couldn't stand up straight for several days. There was no prize, but I didn't care. For once, I finally measured up and felt special. But it wouldn't last long. My life's next chapter was waiting to show its ugly face.

•

BACK AT HOME, I got bored fast. After a couple of days, I was waiting until Mom and Dad were in bed so I could sneak out of the house. I got the chance that night. On my way, I took a couple of my dad's Camels from the pack on the mantelpiece, grabbed a handful of matches from the box in the kitchen, then I left through the back door.

Our stucco house was the only one of its kind in the neighborhood. To the left and right of it were long, ranch-style brick homes. The neighbors on our left had an older girl in college, a younger girl of eight or nine, and a boy named Bob, who was three years older than me. On our right lived was a retired couple who rented out a small cottage at the back of their property. We heard a couple of newlyweds had recently moved in.

I decided I'd head for the railroad tracks—I liked to see how long I could keep my balance without falling off. To get there, I had to pass the cottage, and as I did so, I noticed a light on. As I got closer, I saw it was coming from the bedroom window. When I got close enough to look inside, I almost pissed my pants. At the foot of the bed stood a young lady wearing nothing but her panties. Her breasts, the size of grapefruits, pointed straight out, and her dark nipples were the size of a fifty-cent piece.

I was hidden in the darkness, three or four feet away. Continuing to stare, I started to creep closer to the edge of the window, for a better view. The closer I got, the better she looked. Finally, I got close enough to see black hair bulging beneath her white panties. I was praying she'd take them off.

"Come to bed," I heard her husband say.

Suddenly, up comes Fuzzy, panting and snorting. I ducked just in time. I could tell they heard something.

"I'm going outside to take a look around," said the man.

I pushed Fuzzy away, and he moved off, continuing to sniff and snort. I thought about running down the path, but I was afraid I wouldn't get out of sight fast enough, so I ran and hid under a large honeysuckle bush. It was dark, and the man didn't have a flashlight. I watched him as he walked around the cottage. Afraid Fuzzy would approach me again, I decided to break for the path and run as hard as I could for the railroad tracks.

Again, I'd got a hard-on just looking at a woman. Fear was part of the excitement. This time, it felt like Christmas, my birthday, and the Fourth of July all wrapped up into one. After I'd managed to escape, I walked down the railway tracks smoking and laughing out loud until I reached Cedar Lane, at which point I walked back to my house the long way, afraid to go back the way I came. I'd go past that window many times, but I only saw the lady again one time, and that was a few days later.

I'd hitchhiked into Vienna to check out the new stores in the strip mall. Hitchhiking was easy during the day. On the way back, my first a ride took me a little over a mile up Park Street, five miles from home. I started walking, turning and putting out my thumb whenever I heard a car coming. At one point, I heard a car behind me, and turned and put out my thumb; as the car got closer, I realized it was the lady from the cottage. I was so embarrassed I just dropped my arm and kept on walking, pretending I hadn't been hitching for a ride, but she pulled over on the shoulder right in front of me. I was nervous. Had she seen me spying on her? I walked over to the car.

"Get in," she said through the open window. "I'll give you a ride home."

I sat there in complete silence for the entire five miles. When she pulled up to the row of mailboxes in front of my house, all I could say was, "Thanks." That was the last time I would ever see her, but even today, I like to imagine she saw me watching her, and picked me up because she wanted to have sex with me.

Two days later, I did something frightening.

The kid next door, Bob, was a cool guy. He was a high-school student who played Varsity baseball and football. Sometimes he invited me to play catch in his back yard. That's when Bob told me his family went naked at home. I thought of them as "indoor nudists," a term I made up—I didn't know if there was real name for how they lived. Occasionally, when I knocked on Bob's door, I had to wait for everyone to cover up before I could go inside.

One day, Bob's Mom opened the door and told me to go wait in the living room, as Bob was still in his room getting dressed. She left me in the company of Bob's nine-year-old sister Jenny, who was sitting on the couch in a pink bathrobe. She smiled and motioned for me to sit next to her, and that's when I did something I can't understand, even now. I don't know what got into me, but as soon as I sat down beside her, I put my hand right under her robe and touched her crotch. There was no hair, just a small slit of skin between her legs. She didn't move and said nothing. When I heard Bob coming, I took my hand away. I didn't know it at the time, but I'd just committed my first sexual assault.

"Let's go," said Bob, tossing me the football.

We went outside to play. As far as I know, Jenny never spoke about what I'd done to her. I didn't realize, at the time, I'd done something so terrible. In fact, I was pleased because now I knew what a girl had between her legs—nothing! As far as I could tell, there was just a little slit of skin, nothing more.

Weeks passed, and I managed to stay out of trouble (or managed not to get caught). I finished summer school and started to look forward to starting seventh grade. I couldn't wait to turn thirteen. There was something special about being a teenager. Even better, I'd be starting at a new Junior High school called Henry David Thoreau, just a couple of miles up Cedar Lane. I met a boy my age whose brother worked there at night as a janitor, and he let us drive his old car around the parking lot. I finally got good at driving a stick shift.

At home, things weren't so great. My dad was still drinking. He drank all day while he was working, and got home tired and hung over. The moment he walked in the door, he started hurling threats around. He yelled at Mom because his dinner wasn't ready, or because something was out of place or dirty. He'd come home, eat then go to bed, so we all had to be quiet. We couldn't play, watch TV or listen to the radio.

Dad would punch Mom and me, and sometimes throw

things, but this time his verbal abuse had become more painful than his physical assaults. I hated being at home when he was in the house, so I was always wandering around the neighborhood. Seeing the lady naked had been so exciting, I kept hoping to see another. I started looking into people's windows at night. Several times, I climbed up on the fuel oil tank under our bathroom window and waited for Mom to take a shower, but she always made sure the windows were covered.

Once, I was lurking around outside hoping to see something exciting when I saw Bob's older sister in the bathroom of the house next door. There was an outdoor water spigot right under the bathroom window, so I stepped on it and pulled myself up to look inside. Bob's sister was just stepping out of the shower, but her body was a blur because the window was all steamed up. I jumped down and went around to the other side of the house, where her bedroom was. There were venetian blinds in the window that were almost closed, but there was enough light in the cracks for me to see Bob's sister, who had her back to me when she took off her blue terry cloth robe and dropped it on the bed. "Turn around, turn around," I kept thinking, desperate to see everything. My dick was throbbing, and I felt there was something I should do to it, but what? I unzipped my pants, pulled it out, and began stroking it up and down like the babysitter had.

That was a frustrating evening. When Bob's sister turned around, she was wearing her bra and panties, and I realized I wasn't going to see anything else. I didn't know how to masturbate properly, so I didn't finish the job. I'd also never heard the phrase "Peeping Tom," and I had no idea that it was a crime to sneak around and look in people's windows. Luckily, I stopped doing it after a couple of months, when I discovered something even better.

•

ONE NIGHT, on my way back from roaming round the neighborhood, I was crossing Bob's back yard when I heard someone call my name. It scared me at first, until I saw Bob, sitting in the back seat of his Dad's car.

"Come here. Get in the car," he said.

"What are you doing?" I was worried he might have seen me looking into someone's windows.

"Jerking off. Wanna watch?"

I pretended to not know what he was talking about.

"What are you doing?" I asked again.

"I said I'm jerking off, you little shit. Don't you know what that is?

"Yeah," I said.

"Oh yeah?"

"Yeah." I had no idea what he was talking about.

"Show me," he said.

"Show you what?"

"Show me how you jerk off, stupid."

"You first."

Bob said nothing, but pulled his pants and underwear down to his knees. His dick was already hard. Right away, I noticed he was circumcised. There was lots of dark hair on his thighs, and curly hair around his dick and balls.

I watched exactly what he did so I could copy him and do the same. He held his hand loosely around his dick and moved it up and down. At first, he did it slowly, then he started doing it faster and faster.

I kept watching, wondering what was going to happen. Finally, he stopped, turned his whole body toward me and pointed his dick in my direction.

"Here," he said. "Watch." I looked closely at his dick and something started squirting out. It scared me. It wasn't piss; it looked more like the stuff that comes out of your nose when you've got a cold. Some of it landed on my pants, and the rest went on the seat covers. While it came out, Bob cursed and made strange noises. When it was over, he stopped, reached down and picked up an old T-shirt that he used to wipe off his dick. Then he pulled up his pants and threw me the T-shirt.

"Your turn."

Too embarrassed to pull down my pants, I reached in and pulled out my soft dick. I pulled back the foreskin and started to move it up and down. It felt weird to have Bob there, watching me.

"Get on with it," he said. "What's the matter with you?"

I did everything I'd seen him do, but nothing was happening. He started telling me what to do and how to do it, but it didn't make a difference.

"Look," he said. "I'll show you." He put one of his hands on my dick and the other under my balls. He moved his hand up and down a couple of times, and my dick started to get hard. He was doing the same thing Joanie had done. It started to feel good.

"Put it in your mouth," I said.

"Hell no, I don't do that," said Bob. "No way. Forget it." He got out of the car and went inside without another word. I walked home feeling confused and inadequate. So much was happening in my life, nothing seemed to be going the way it should.

•

ONE HOT AFTERNOON, I was riding my bike near Westview Elementary School. There was a long hill by the school that gave you over a mile of downhill riding, with no pedaling. On the way back, it was easier to just walk your bike up the hill; it was too far and too hard to pedal.

I was almost at the top of the hill when I saw a black girl on her bike speeding past me. She reminded me of Joanie, but I knew it wasn't her. For some dumb reason—to this day I still don't understand why—as she sped by me, I yelled: "Nigger!"

Slowly, the girl turned her bike around and started pedaling up the hill toward me. I didn't know what to do or say. I just stood there holding my bike until she got to me. When she did so, she dropped her bike, walked up to me, grabbed mine from my hands and threw it in the ditch.

"What did you say?" she said, and without waiting for a reply, she slapped me hard across the face. I stumbled backwards and tripped into the ditch. She pounced on top of me and began hitting me, repeating over and over: "What did you say?" each time she hit me. All I could manage to say was: "Stop it."

She continued until she got tired. I didn't fight back. It wouldn't have made any difference if I had. I was better off just trying to cover myself.

To cut a long story short, I got my ass beaten by a girl. As she picked up her bike, she said: "Next time you better think twice before you call somebody that name."

The girl might have temporarily crushed my delicate ego, but looking back, I can't help but admire her. She really taught me a lesson.

•

THE NEXT DAY I rode my bike down the same road to Merrifield, about six miles from my house. I'd heard a horse riding stable had just opened, and I thought I might get a job there. The sign next to the road read: "Merrifield Riding Stable, horses rented by the hour, all equipment included." At the bottom, there was a smaller sign: "HELP WANTED." But when I asked the manager about the job, he told me I was too young, and it would be against the law to hire me. I kept begging him. "I'll do anything," I said.

Finally, he asked me to follow him. We walked to the barn.

"Do you really like horses?" he asked.

"Sure Mister. I've always wanted a horse of my own."

"Well," he says, "meet Butler. He's blind in the right eye, and he's old, but the kids love him. I'll make a deal with you. If you work every weekend for the rest of the summer without pay, I'll let you have Butler, and he'll be all yours."

It never crossed my mind to wonder how and where I'd keep a horse, much less how much it would cost to feed one. I was so excited, I just kept saying, "Yes sir. Yes sir."

"The head groom is Andy. He'll tell you everything you need to know. Just report to Andy every weekend. By October, you'll have your own horse."

The work wasn't really so bad. The hardest part was cleaning the horseshit out of the stalls and spreading hay around. When the riders brought the horses in, I'd take them for a short ten minute walk to cool them down, then, I'd take off their saddles and blankets, take them to their stall and remove their bridles. I always checked to see if they had any cuts or wounds, and make sure they still had all four shoes. Sometimes I'd brush them, but I didn't need to wash or groom them. That happened during the week.

Butler was a gentle horse, mostly gray, who could still see well despite being semi-blind. Most of the time, young children would ride him, but some weekends he needed exercising, so I'd get to take him out for a run. Fuzzy would come with us. Those two were getting friendly.

The weeks passed quickly. I was surprised how important Butler and the stable became to me. My mom didn't know about my deal with the manager. She thought I was just helping out and getting free horse rides in exchange.

That year, I turned thirteen, and when summer ended I was going to start junior high school. My mom and dad continued to argue, but I stayed away from them as much as I could, so they didn't notice I'd managed to stay out of trouble all summer. But I wasn't thinking about trouble; I was only thinking about Butler. I'd met a man who owned a couple of acres of land near Merrifield where he raised chickens and a couple of cows. He was willing to keep Butler for me as long as I paid for his food and vet bills. I agreed, without having any idea how much any of it would cost.

On Saturday, a week before school started—the week before I was supposed to get Butler—I rode my bike down the short road that led to the barn, and right away I noticed the sign advertising the riding stables had gone.

I got off my bike and walked up to Andy.

"What's up, kid?" he said.

"Where's the sign?"

"They're all gone," said Andy.

"What do you mean? Gone where?" I looked toward the barn and saw it was empty. Usually, at this time of day, horses were being saddled and riders were setting out.

"They all left, kid, they're gone. The stable's closed till next summer."

"Where's Butler?"

"Gone with them."

"No! He's supposed to be my horse!"

Finally, it began to settle into my mind what had happened. Angry tears began to fall down my cheeks, but there was nothing I could do but go home.

Soledad

San Quentin

2

FRAGMENTS

PRISON BITCH

WHEN I WAS 14, I ran away from home again, and was arrested in for stealing a car in Washington, D.C. The cops knew exactly how old I was. They didn't care. The night I was arrested, they took me from the police station to a D.C. jail, where they put me in a big room with lots of bunk beds. The room was full of men, most of them black. I was a skinny little kid.

I was so scared that all I could think about was trying to survive. I did whatever they told me to. I didn't think twice.

They raped me all night. They called me "white bitch." It felt as if I was being punished for something. I can't remember how many guys raped me that night, but my best guess is between forty and fifty. Some of them just wanted to fuck me, some wanted me to suck their dicks, but most of them wanted me to do both. I tried not to make eye contact with any of them, and just listened to what they told me. I stayed as passive as possible.

All night, it was a repeat of the same things again and again. I was abused, threatened, and humiliated. I was slapped, punched, pissed on, spit on, fucked in the ass, forced to swallow piss, and made to taste my own shit. Strangely, the words scared and hurt me more than the physical acts.

I had no idea what time it was, but it was probably around three or four in the morning when the last guy finished with me, and left me alone in the bathroom. I turned on the shower and tried to see what they'd done to me. A toe on my right foot was broken. My knees were cut and scraped. There was a cut inside my mouth where I'd bitten myself when someone slapped me in the face, and blood ran down the inside of my legs. There was a bump on my forehead where I'd been pushed into the wall.

I opened the dirty white plastic curtain and got out of the stall. A slim black guy was waiting for me, holding my towel and jumpsuit. He put one hand behind my neck and pulled me towards him, reaching for my dick with his other hand. He kissed me on the mouth. Since he was skinny and around my height, I thought about pushing him away, but I was too scared and exhausted. He told me to dry off and put my jumpsuit on. He asked me if I was okay. I was afraid to speak, so I just nodded. Then he took me back to his bunk, which was in the furthest, darkest corner of the room.

This guy, who had a reddish tone to his skin, told me to call him Tangerine. He said he was going to show me what to do. He told me to get undressed and to get into his bed. He told me that if I didn't want them to hurt me, I had to act as though I liked what they were doing. For the next two hours, Tangerine pimped me out to guys who wanted to fuck me but hadn't wanted to do it in the bathroom with the others.

They paid him in cigarettes, candy bars, or cookies. A few of the guys who'd just raped me paid to fuck me again. I lay on my stomach and tried not to see their faces. There was no more pain. My asshole was completely dead. Tangerine would let me take a break now and then to smoke a cigarette or eat a candy bar. Around 5 a.m., when everybody was asleep, I wiped away the blood, dressed in my jumpsuit, and went and sat on the floor by the door, waiting for the cops to come and get me.

Eventually, they got me and took me back to Virginia. I didn't talk to them, or anyone else, for several days. They took me to a jail in Alexandria, booked me, and put me in a cell by myself. I'd been up all night, and I was exhausted. I immediately went to sleep.

That jail had sections, and there were five or six cells in each section. There were two other guys in my section. While I was asleep, one of them took a razor, reached through the bars in front of my cell, and shaved the peach fuzz off one of my arms. When I woke up and saw what they'd done, I was scared, not knowing who'd done it, or why. There was a radio playing during the day and most of the night, and I tried to concentrate on the sound from the radio. I still didn't speak. When they took me to court, the judge ordered that I be tested to determine whether I was competent to stand trial. I was taken to a hospital. I didn't speak to anyone there, either, but they still found me competent. The judge gave me one year.

The guards at the Alexandria jail offered me the job of working sanitation in the Work Release section of the jail.

The Work Release section was one big room with twenty-four beds, but there were never more than twelve men there, as the other twelve would be out on Work Release. In that section, the bunks were bigger than in the rest of the jail. The bathroom was clean, and there was a small kitchen with a refrigerator. I would be on my own for several hours every day, and I figured I'd have the place to myself. It sounded like a good deal, so I took it.

I was wrong. Soon after starting work there, I became the Work Release bitch. The men shaved my body so that my skin was smooth, and they dressed me in panties and lipstick. I decided not to fight back. During the year, at least two hundred men passed through the Work Release section, and more than half of them fucked me. Eventually, I became submissive and effeminate, and no one had to threaten me or hurt me in order to have sex with them. This is how I became a woman.

There were some who didn't like being around me, and there were some who didn't like seeing or knowing about what I was doing, but I left the privacy issue up to the person who was fucking me. If they wanted privacy, we'd hang an army blanket in front of the bunk, covering us from sight. A lot of them didn't care, and I'd suck their dick or let them fuck me out in the open, anywhere in the room. It was a turn-on to have guys watching me suck dick.

What I remember most about that year at the Alexandria jail was how hard I tried to please everybody. During the day, when I wasn't making beds, washing clothes, or keeping everything clean, I was always looking for ways to make myself more like a woman. The guards knew what was going on, and never said or did anything to discourage me.

I began giving myself enemas every day, sometimes twice or three times a day. I got so I could tell when there was shit in my ass, and I always got it out. When there's a lot of hard shit taking up space in your ass, it causes more pain when a dick is being pushed up inside you.

I also worked on stretching my asshole. I'd sit on coke bottles and other things. Sometimes I ripped myself by accident. I got my asshole to be loose as a pussy. There were very few dicks I couldn't take. Nothing could hurt me. I could easily take seven or eight inches without feeling any pain, but no matter what size it was, I always wanted to take the whole dick. The largest I ever saw must have been at least a foot long when it was hard, and seven or eight inches soft. Yes, it was a black guy. I've known some white guys with big dicks, but in general, black guys are bigger. Of course, I tried to get the whole twelve inches in my ass. I lay on the bed with a couple of pillows under my stomach, pushing my ass in the air. I tried pushing back when he was pushing in, but it just wasn't going to happen. The guy didn't care whether he got his whole dick inside me or not—he just wanted to cum. So, for the record, the most I've had inside me is about ten inches.

Most of the guys I had sex with had medium to small dicks (I call six inches medium—anything less than that is small to me). I enjoyed sucking small dicks more than having them in my ass. A lot of guys would do what was called a "reach-around," which meant they'd fuck me when I was on my side, and they'd reach around and give me a hand job while they were fucking me. Some of them would want to suck my dick, or have me fuck them (if I promised not to tell). I've always liked getting my dick sucked, and I still do, if it's done right, but it's always been difficult for me to fuck another man in the ass. I can get my dick hard enough to get it in, but it just doesn't turn me on enough for it to stay hard.

There were several closet queers and freaks at that jail, but I think most of the guys who wanted to fuck me or suck my dick were first timers—it was only being in jail that caused them to consider having sex with a man. I never needed anything—someone would always get it for me. Lipstick, makeup, panties, stockings... I tried it all. Even though my chest was flat, guys would still want to suck my nipples. Some of them would kiss me, even with their tongues. In time, I developed a female persona.

On the weekends, everyone would get a pass which allowed them to leave, as long as they were back before midnight on Sunday. Some weekends, one or two guys would decide to stay. I couldn't understand why anybody would want to stay in jail. When they did, if it was someone that had fucked me, I'd fantasize that they stayed because they wanted to be alone with me.

That year of my life, when I was fifteen, I had sex every day, sometimes just once or twice, and sometimes up to eight times a day with different guys. Even when I was sick, there was still somebody who wanted to fuck me.

I was seventeen when I left the Alexandria jail. My father came to pick me up and take me home, but I soon ran away again. I knew he wouldn't come after me. I was looking forward to being on my own, and buying my own beer in one of those joints that turned me away when I was a kid.

What followed were years of drinking, smoking pot, burglaries, then marriage.

My first wife's name was Livia. She was four feet eleven inches high, and pretty. She rarely ever initiated sex between us, though she didn't mind sucking my dick—in fact, I think she enjoyed it—she just wouldn't swallow my cum. I tried to get her to swallow it just one time. We were parked outside a 7-11 and she was giving me head. She agreed to swallow half if I would swallow the other half. That was the one and only time she did it. Livia wasn't much into sex, but she did what I wanted just to make me happy. Once she let me fuck her in the ass, but it hurt her so bad that I never tried it again.

For a small girl, Livia had a big pussy. I was always surprised how easily I could get my whole hand half way up inside her. Back then, there wasn't a lot of talk about "fist fucking," but I knew I could probably have got my fist in there if I wanted to. I've always wondered why some women are so big and others are so tight. My dick is about seven inches long and medium thick. I don't know why or how, but she never made a sound when I jammed it up inside her. I tried to hurt her, but I couldn't. At least, not in that way.

But I hurt her in other ways. The last thing I wanted was to become like my father, but that was what seemed to be happening. I became a control freak. I treated Livia as if she was my property. I made her do a lot of stuff she didn't want to do. For example, one day I threw out all her underwear.

I didn't want her wearing any. Livia had very small breasts and didn't really need to wear a bra, but at first, she was very scared and self-conscious when I would lift up her skirt in public and expose her ass. After a while, I think she got used to it. Maybe she even liked the attention. Doing things like that was the only way I could get aroused enough to keep my dick hard. Normal sex wasn't enough for me. It didn't turn me on.

Basically, I preferred sex with men. Where women were concerned, I was an exhibitionist and a Peeping Tom, though I didn't know it at the time. I'd fuck Livia anywhere I thought I could get away with it. I'd get off on watching how people would react. I liked to make them uncomfortable. Once, late at night, we went into a 7-11. I just lifted Livia's little ass up on the counter and fucked her right there in front of the female clerk, who just stood there smiling.

Livia and I decided we wanted to go to California. We took off, taking westbound highways until we hit the Pacific Ocean. The trip was full of drama and crime. When we arrived in California, we didn't have anywhere in particular to go. I got into trouble right away. I pulled several armed robberies and burglaries, and we went on the run. I attacked a guy, hitting him over the head with a wine bottle, which left him badly injured. I shot another guy in the leg. I sexually assaulted a woman during a burglary. Things got bad. The cops were soon after me. They set up a roadblock to try and stop me, and it all ended in a big shootout in Glendale.

It was January 1967, and I was 19 years old. They took me to a jail in Santa Monica. From there, they took me to the

L.A. County Jail. I was kept in solitary until I went to court for sentencing. The judge gave me five years to life, and told me I'd have to do at least forty months before I was eligible for parole. Then I was taken to the Chino Guidance Center to be evaluated and classified. Then they sent me to Tracy, a prison for first offenders who were under twenty-one. That was how I ended up doing time in California.

SLAVE OF SAN QUENTIN

I EXPERIENCED SO MUCH sex and violence at Soledad and San Quentin that, for a long time, I wondered how to write about the years I spent as a prisoner and slave in those jails. In the end, I realized that, since a lot of my sexual experiences were filthy and dirty, they need to be described that way. So, I decided just to tell the truth, in the language I'm familiar with.

I've been fucked in the ass by at least four or five hundred different guys, likely more. My memory stops after about fifty. After that, I only remember those that stood out. Sometimes today, I think back into my past to someone who might only have fucked me once or twice. I have no physical memory of it, but there's still a vague trace of an intimate experience we shared.

When I got to Tracy, there were a lot of minimum-security inmates housed temporarily in the gym, since they were working in the fields. A guy about my age began following me and hanging out with me. He told me he was a homosexual and he wanted to be with me. He was afraid that, if he was on his own, it was just a matter of time before someone would claim him to be their bitch.

He was right. Before long, guys started approaching my boy, offering to pay him for sex. He was quick to tell them that he belonged to me, even though I hadn't had sex with him myself. I told him to go ahead and make us some money.

We had a good thing going for a while, but it didn't last long. I didn't know it, but my cell buddy was planning to escape. One day, the guards did a random shakedown of our cell, and they found two hacksaw blades. I had no idea they were there, but my cell buddy said they were mine. My denials were pointless. They put me in lock-up, eventually transferring me to Soledad Central.

My stay at Soledad was cut short. A major riot broke out within two weeks of my arrival. Some were killed, and many more were hurt. Our tier was gassed, and the officer in charge was killed. They put several inmates on segregation for investigation, including me, although I had nothing to do with the riot. After thirty days, I was reclassified and sent to my new home.

I got to San Quentin in late 1967. I went through the regular intake system and was given a new prison number: B-10632. Since I'd come from Soledad with a bad rap, they put me on solitary lock-up for thirteen months.

Looking back at this time, even though I'd grown into an adult physically, I was still a juvenile in terms of mental and emotional maturity. Only now do I understand how terrified I was. I had no self-worth or self-esteem. Even now, I still don't understand what made me want to keep going, but I did. I guess people will do anything to survive.

That stretch of three and a half years at San Quentin was the most sexually active time of my life. I was always somebody's bitch, and I was too scared to say no. When guys demanded sex, I wasn't sure how far I needed to go, so I just went all the way. Being a prison bitch was no different from being a slave, or a prisoner-of-war. If I'd resisted, somebody would have killed me long ago.

It took a while, but I learned to like having sex with men, and then, at some point, I became addicted to it. I haven't really tried to analyze it, but I know that the thing that gives me the most pleasure in the world is sucking dick. I really don't know why this is, but it reminds me of how a baby is comforted by sucking and chewing on a pacifier. I think my love of dick isn't just sexual. At some level, it also gives me a feeling of comfort and safety.

Another reason why I had so much sex at San Quentin was due to the drug habit I'd developed, and needed to support. I started by using heroin, but I also did a lot of LSD, weed, hash, and speed. Some of the drugs I did, I didn't even know what they were. This was before AIDS, but still, when I look back and think about some of the risks I took, I know I should have been dead long ago.

It was an interesting time to be at San Quentin. In February 1969, when I'd been there a year and a half, Johnny Cash played a live concert at the prison. The cons all loved him, especially his big hit at the time, "A Boy Named Sue." After the concert, he donated fifty thousand dollars to the prison inmates' fund. In April that year, they brought in Charles Manson and put him on death row, where he was joined a month later by Sirhan Sirhan, Robert F. Kennedy's assassin, though neither of them were executed, as the death penalty in California was repealed. Then, right before I left, there was a big shootout. The infamous George Jackson, founder of the Black Guerrilla Family (a major African-American prison gang) had been brought to the prison after killing a guard at Soledad. In August 1971 he tried to escape, taking a number of hostages. Jackson and five other inmates were shot and killed.

I spent my first thirteen months at San Quentin in the segregation block, which was on south side of B-block. In segregation, there were five tiers, with fifty single cells to a tier, which made two hundred and fifty men. I was on the third tier, and my cell faced the ocean, though I couldn't see it. The orderly on our tier was a tall slim black guy with a reddish complexion. As soon as I got there, he came straight to my cell. He brought me two standard-issue army-style blankets, two sheets, a washcloth, a roll of toilet paper, a bar of state soap, and a small brown envelope that contained tooth powder. He said he was giving me an extra blanket "free of charge" because it was going to get real cold in a couple of months. He told me to call him Chicken. I learned he had a life sentence for murder. I never asked why he was on segregation, but I knew he'd been there a long time. Since he was the orderly, his cell was open all day.

It might sound funny coming from me, but Chicken was a freak. The second day I was there, he came to my cell, called me over to the bars, and went straight for my dick, rubbing it through the front of my pants. Then he unbuttoned them, let them drop to the ground, pulled down my underpants, and started stroking my dick. When it got hard, he told me to lie down on my bunk so he could watch me finish. Without a word, I lay down and quickly felt my own cum explode on my stomach and chest. That was how it began with me and Chicken.

Chicken knew I'd already been "turned out," which was the term used to describe someone who'd been fucked in the ass. He knew it right away, the first time I got his dick in my mouth. Chicken's dick was pretty long. He could stand outside my cell and still have five or six inches through the bars on the other side. It was thin and reddish in color, like his skin, and he was uncircumcised, like me. When his dick was hard and he skinned it back, the head would be almost as red as the top of a dog's dick.

It had been a while since I'd been with anyone, and the first time I sucked Chicken's dick, it turned on all the bitch desires in me. After that first time, Chicken was at the bars of my cell every day for three or four hours every day. I wanted his dick in my mouth all the time, and he wanted mine, but he wouldn't suck my dick through the bars because he knew all the other guys on the tier were watching us through their little pieces of mirror. He didn't want anyone to know he was "taking it." Still, every time I would cum, he wanted to eat it. Sometimes he'd jerk me off and ask me to cum in his hand, and when I did, he'd walk away and go back to his cell to lick his hand.

In the segregation block, we were locked in our cells twenty-four hours a day. Once a week, we were let out one at a time to take a shower. We had to shower quickly. We called it taking a bird bath, or a whore's bath. You step under the water, get wet, get your wash rag wet, soap yourself up, then step back under the water and rinse off. The showers were timed, and when the shower timer went off, you had to go back to your cell.

Some guys didn't bother taking showers. Instead, they would use the time to go and talk to a buddy, shoot the shit, and trade books or magazines. I would always watch them and hope they'd come down to my cell, and a lot of them did. There were about ten guys who would regularly give up their shower time to get their dicks sucked. Soon I started to get extra food and books to read as payment for my services. If I'd been a woman, I'd certainly have been a complete slut.

When the guards yelled "Lock in!," everybody had to get back to their cell within two minutes, whether they'd showered or not. The guards were different then. We never called them Correctional Officers, like we do now. We called them Guards, Pigs, Hacks, or Bulls. Unlike C.O.s today, they didn't pay any attention to what you did when you were out of your cell.

We could only take our towels and shower shoes with us when we showered. Most guys would tie their towels around their waist when they walked down the tier, but I always walked there naked. On shower days, I would stay naked in my cell all day, except in the winter. I was 20, but I looked and acted 16, and got a lot of attention, which always got me off. I loved teasing the guys. Chicken didn't care if I wanted to suck another guy's dick. But I didn't just want to suck one other guy's dick, I wanted to suck the dick of every guy on the tier—everybody except for this one guy who used to throw piss and shit through the bars of my cell every time he passed by. He stopped doing it when Chicken talked to him, but he'd still spit on me. This guy caused me a lot of trouble later, when Chicken wasn't there to protect me.

Anyway, before that first week was out, everyone on the tier knew I was a bitch, although they didn't know I was Chicken's bitch. During the thirteen months I was on segregation, I sucked his dick every day, whether he wanted me to or not, except for shower day, when I sucked a lot of other guys' dicks. I had that Chicken wrapped around my little finger. He'd do anything he could for me, given the confines of the tier. He especially liked to play with my dick, get it hard, then have me lay down on my bunk and jack off while he watched me. At that age, I could recover within minutes.

I could always make Chicken cum, and whenever I did, I'd play with him by keeping his cum in my mouth, then freak him out by opening my mouth and showing it to him. That was typical of the kind of thing that amused me back then. Most of the jokes we told and the humor we shared was around sex. Today it's hard for me to find anything that will make me laugh out loud.

When I look back on it, if I sucked Chicken's dick six times every week, that makes three hundred and thirty-six blow jobs. If I sucked, on average, ten dicks every shower day, that makes another five hundred and sixty. So in total, I gave around eight hundred and ninety-six blow jobs in thirteen months. That would turn out to be nothing compared to what happened to me when I finally got out on population.

I had two six-month classification reviews before they recommended me to be released from segregation, and it took another thirty days to get the Warden's approval. When I finally left the tier, Chicken told me that he knew some guys who were going to look out for me. He said he'd tell me exactly where to go, and if nobody came for me, I should just wait. He told me that everything was going to be alright.

I believe it was around Thanksgiving of 1968 when I stepped outside the south side of B-block. Chicken had told me to wait near the door leading to the upper yard. I'd been standing there less than five minutes when a fat guy in his late 30s came up to me. He had long, unkempt hair and a long beard, and was dressed in a dirty coat and jeans. Not long after that, I got a big surprise. Despite his promises to keep me safe, Chicken had sold me to an Aryan Nation motorcycle gang.

One of the best-kept secrets of San Quentin (and probably all other prisons) is the fact that most of these so-called macho killer-type dudes—the guys who had their own punks or bitches—were also bitches themselves. By this I mean that, more times than not, they wanted their own punks to fuck them, or at least they liked to suck dick. I learned this from the first Aryan Nation dude that owned me.

This guy, like me, was a redhead in his early twenties, but I was light and thin, and this guy was around two hundred and forty pounds, with hair all over his back and even his ass. His dick was only four or five inches long, but fat. The first time I went with him, we were in a cell together, and he hung up an army blanket in front of the bars so no one could see us. I grabbed his dick and stuck the head of it in my mouth, sucking him to try and make him cum. But he didn't want to cum right then. He wanted me to fuck him.

He put grease on his ass to help smooth the way. When he saw that my dick wasn't hard enough, he peered around the army blanket, checking to see if anyone was on the tier, then he started sucking my dick. I remember thinking how strange it was that this big macho killer was down on his knees sucking my dick. Well, it doesn't matter who it is, my dick always gets hard if somebody sucks it. Once it was hard, he told me to fuck him. I managed to get it inside him and stabbed him a few times, but my dick never stays hard from fucking a man in the ass.

The dude must have been through this situation before, because he knew what to do. He kept getting up and sucking my dick to get it hard, then he'd accept whatever I could manage to do before it got soft again. Still, it was no good. Neither of us could cum that way, and he ended up jerking off while I watched. I don't exactly know why, but I felt sorry for the dude.

In the late 1960s and early 1970s, there was a lot of violence and killing at San Quentin. In the summer of 1970, I saw a guy die in front of me. We were on lockdown, and I was in my cell, talking to a kitchen worker through the bars (guys who worked in the kitchens didn't have to be locked down). Suddenly, these black guys dropped down over the side of the fourth tier and started stabbing him. He just fell to the ground right in front of my cell. There was nothing I could do. I just stood there and watched him bleed out on the ground.

The dead guy's cell buddy was also a kitchen worker, and he was working in the kitchen at the time. When he came back to his cell and found out what had happened, it really fucked him up. He kept saying, "I should have come back with him." He was trained in Martial Arts, and he knew that if he'd been there, the black guys would probably have chosen someone else to kill.

Two weeks later, we all came off lockdown, including the dead guy's cell buddy, who hadn't been back to work since the killing. After finishing work that day, he went into the shower and there were five black guys in there. I heard this guy went stone cold crazy on them. No one was killed, but he beat them all severely. This led to another two-week lockdown. When we came off this lockdown, the whole jail was tense. Everybody was waiting for the retaliation, and it soon came. Two old white guys were stabbed on the bleachers in the lower yard, and one of them was killed.

I only belonged to the Aryan Nation dude for a few days, until word got around that I'd been sucking black dicks while I was on lock-up. Needless to say, that was an embarrassment to the Aryan Nation gang. They sold me to a gang of Mexicans for fifty dollars' worth of heroin. The rest of the time I was there, I was owned by this gang, which numbered between fifty and seventy-five members at San Quentin alone, and a lot more spread out over the Californian prison system. They were known as the San Antonio Family, and they were heavily involved in smuggling and selling drugs, which is how I started using. There were lots of fights, stabbings, and murders in this gang. I'd get beaten up if I didn't do what I was told, or if I did something wrong.

I belonged to a guy named Cuervo. I called him by his English name, Crow. He was only around 25 or 26, but he was already one of the high-level gang leaders. Once again, I'd come to learn that this was a man who liked the dick. His body, like mine, was smooth, with very little hair. At first, I was somewhat attracted to him. He had a baby face, and lips just like a girl's. My dick would get hard just from kissing him. Crow only fucked me once, and I fucked him a few times, but mostly we got off on sucking each other's dicks, usually at the same time. Crow let me have sex with anyone I wanted to. He wasn't possessive. Looking back, things would have been better for me if he was.

I belonged to Crow for about three years. Pretty soon, he started to get me high on heroin. At one point, he got me high every day for about a week, and it felt so good that I didn't want to come back down. Crow got me hooked, and while I was with him, I became a drug addict. When Crow scored big, he kept me high, but there were times when things would dry up and I'd have to go out and score for myself. Crow used occasionally, but he never got addicted. He and his crew were always struggling and fighting to maintain their control of the heroin market in the joint.

When the Mexican gang sent me to Crow, I was in the

south block. I was told it would take a few days to get me transferred to his cell, which was in the east block. In 1968, San Quentin was segregated in the sense that whites and blacks were never put in the same cell, although whites and Mexicans were often put together. After I'd been on population for a month or so, while waiting to move to the east block, I got assigned to the laundry as a clerk. I had to check with Crow to see if that was okay with him, and he told me to go and see what it was all about.

I found out I was going to be working in the office that overlooked the laundry. About twenty guys worked there, all blacks. The old man supervising me said I could take it easy. I had a desk to myself and my own typewriter (I had no idea how to type). There were no guards in the laundry, which had its own bathrooms and showers downstairs, underneath the office where I worked.

The old man told me that the shift ended at 2 p.m., at which time everyone who worked in the laundry, including me, had to take a shower. We had to be out by 2:30 to return to our cell blocks. He told me that I should take my shower earlier, to avoid having to shower with all the black guys. His advice was no help. Although I'd recently turned 21, I still looked 17. It was the hippie era, and I wore my hair down to my shoulders. As soon as I got undressed and stepped into the shower, a bunch of black guys followed me.

That shower was real big, with at least ten showerheads. It was pretty clean, but it was dark, with only two 25 watt bulbs to light the whole room. Despite my fear, I put a smile on my face and did what they asked me to do. I'd learned my lesson from the D.C. jail. I don't know how many guys there were, but I figured they were all going to want to cum. I realized the quickest way to do that would be to suck them all off. I hadn't counted on the fact that some of them would want more than a quick blowjob.

My second day at the laundry, I was confronted by a guy with a knife who threatened to stab me if I didn't let him fuck me. I decided to let him. If I resisted, and he stabbed me, there would have been big trouble with Crow. There would have been a fight, and somebody might have gotten killed. But if it was just sex, then Crow didn't care. It didn't matter to him how many guys I fucked or sucked off, whether they paid me for it or not, just as long as I didn't have sex with any of his homies. Go figure.

After three and a half years at San Quentin, I was given a parole date, my security level was lowered, and I was sent to a prison in the mountains called Tehachapi to get ready for my release, which was less than three months away. Crow let his San Antonio homies know I was coming, and they met me at the Receiving and Release building when I got off the bus. I was their property until I left.

At Tehachapi, nobody had more than 18 months to serve. There was only one fence and no gun towers. The only time I can remember seeing any guards was at shift change, when they came in to take the count. It was nothing like San Quentin. Tehachapi had a four-hole golf course, basketball courts, handball courts, a large track, and a gym where they showed movies on the weekends. Very few inmates had jobs. I didn't work the whole time I was there.

I spent most of my time by myself, at the gym or track, or on the golf course. I still got high every day. I took whatever I could get. The guy who owned me for the next three months was a buddy of Crow's called Nino, a kid around the same age as me, 21 or 22 at most. As soon as I got to Tehachapi, he put me through a special initiation, after which he became my pimp, and he worked me every night until I left.

In order to make parole, I had to agree that I'd return to Virginia to live with my parents. Of course, they had to agree to it as well. I hated the idea of going back there, and I'm sure my parents felt the same way, but however bad it got, I figured it couldn't be any worse than prison.

Rapist

I STAYED OUT OF PRISON from the early summer of 1972 until mid-1975. Those three years were the longest period of time I'd been out of prison since I was ten years old.

I didn't know it at the time, but I left California with a need to accomplish certain things. I really wanted to stay out of prison. I wanted to fit in somewhere. I wanted to become a different person. For the last five-and-a-half years, I'd been in the control of other people. They had set the boundaries. They'd made me who and what I was. Now, I needed to forget my past. My driving ambition was to create a new identity and personality. I had to go from being a mindless jailhouse bitch to being a real man. And for this, I needed a woman.

I worked for a while in my father's house-painting business, and saw my parole officer every week. Eventually, I got permission to move and change jobs. I trained as a carpenter. My job meant I often had to stay over at job sites in Maryland, only returning to Virginia when the work was done. Before long, I started smoking weed. After working all day, I'd go drinking in Georgetown at night. I spent all my time and money at a crowded little club called the Crazy Horse on J Street. That's where I met Donna.

Like my first wife, Donna was short—around four feet eleven. She was pretty, perky, and always seemed happy. We both worked hard all day and met up every night at the Crazy Horse, where we'd drink, dance, and laugh. It didn't take long for me to fall in love with her smile and her happiness. Donna liked to drink, sometimes heavily, but she didn't smoke pot. At first, I was more interested in hanging out with her than fucking her, so I didn't put her under any pressure. I didn't make a sexual move on her for weeks. In time, I learned that this was why she liked me. By then, we were married, and it was too late.

My life became a routine. I'd work during the day, then meet up with Donna and go to the Crazy Horse, where we'd drink and smoke pot. I became very sexually frustrated, because Donna didn't want to fuck, but she didn't want me to go with any other women. We'd make out in the car every night. She liked to kiss. She liked it when I played with her tits, and she liked me to spend a lot of time eating her pussy, but she didn't like to suck my dick. I got her to do it now and then, but I could tell she didn't enjoy it.

I was in my mid-twenties when I got married again. I only tried to fuck Donna once, and that was the night of our honeymoon. Her pussy was very small and very tight. When I tried to enter her, she pulled away and told me it hurt too much. I turned her over and tried her ass, but the result was the same. I told her it was okay. I said I was willing to accept her as she was. That was how badly I needed her.

Somehow, I managed to convince myself that she loved me as much as I loved her, but at some level I knew it wasn't true. Our marriage didn't last long. One night in the Crazy Horse, she told me it was over between us.

That night, I committed my first rape.

I'd hurt women before, and assaulted them sexually, but I'd never actually raped anyone until then. I left Donna in the Crazy Horse around 2:15 a.m. and just began to drive. I hit 495 and drove into Maryland. I was scared and confused, and I drove until the sun came up. At some point, I realized I was running out of gas, and I had no money apart from a few coins in my pocket. I needed gas to get back to Virginia so I could go to work in the morning. I started to get worried, and made the decision to break into someone's house and look for cash. I left my car in a motel parking lot and walked to a nearby residential area.

I chose a house at random. I knocked on the front door. I was planning to threaten the homeowner with violence and ask them for money, but no one answered. I tried the door. It was locked, so I went around to the back and got inside through a sliding glass screen, which was open. Once I was in the kitchen, I took a steak knife out of the silverware drawer and went to explore the house. In the living room I came face-to-face with a young girl who'd obviously been woken up by my knocking at the door. She was around eighteen, and was dressed in a see-through nightdress, panties and a bra.

I was angry to find the house was occupied, as it meant my crime was far more serious. I asked the girl for money. She told me she didn't have any. I threatened her with the knife, and when I realized how terrified she was, I found myself getting extremely turned on in a very surprising and unusual way. I raped her.

After the rape, I tied the girl up and had just started searching the house for money or valuables when her mother walked in the front door. When she saw me, she became frantic. I told her I needed money, and she went to her bedroom right away, and came back with a little over a hundred dollars—more than enough to get me back home. Once again, the control I had over the woman, and her fear, got me very aroused. This woman was in her mid-forties, and stronger than the girl. She tried to resist me verbally, but when I told her what I was going to do to her, she obviously realized she had no choice.

I fucked both women without a rubber. My dick stayed unusually hard throughout both rapes. It felt wonderful!

I raped a lot more women after that. It always went the same way. I'd go to a neighborhood. When I saw a man leaving for work in the morning, I'd wait for a while, then knock on the door of his house. If a woman answered, I'd tell her I was interested in buying the property, and ask if I could take a look around. If she let me in, I'd pull out a butcher's knife and threaten her with it, then I'd lock the door and tell her to go and get all her cash. None of my victims had any more than $200. Then I'd tell them to take me to the bedroom.

I told them that if they cooperated with me and did what I

said, I wouldn't hurt them. But if they tried to fight back, I'd have to hurt them and maybe kill them. That would terrify them. None of them screamed, talked back to me, tried to hurt me, or tried to escape. If they had, I would have had to hurt them to regain my control.

When we got to the bedroom, I'd tell them to take off their clothes one piece of clothing at a time, and hand me each item after taking it off. Having to undress and stand naked in front of me always made them even more fearful, and got me more excited. I'd grab one of their hands, put their hand on my dick and tell them to start stroking. When I felt I might cum soon, I'd stop them, grab their arms tightly and walk or pull them to the bathroom. Here, I'd give them a choice. I'd say that someone is going to get a "golden shower." One of us is going to get in the bathtub and get pissed on. I gave them the choice to piss on me, or have me piss on them. I would really get off if they chose to piss on me. If I pissed on them, I'd piss all over their head, eyes, face, mouth, tits, stomach, and pussy.

Then I'd take them back into the bedroom. My dick would remain hard all the time. With my dick in hand, I'd point it at them and ask where did they want it first—in the ass, in the mouth, or in the pussy? I told them that whatever they said, it was going to go in all three places. I was asking them to decide the order. The smartest ones chose to leave their ass for last, so they wouldn't have to taste shit in their mouth.

When it came to fucking them in the ass, I got pleasure out of trying to hurt them. I fucked them hard and fast. I deliberately wouldn't cum in their ass. If their shit was hard, it wouldn't stick to my dick, but if it was soft or runny, when I pulled out my dick it would have some of their shit on it. If they asked for it in their pussy second, they were lucky, as the shit would rub off inside their pussy, so when it was time for it to go into their mouth, there wouldn't be anything but pussy juice on it.

I wanted to hurt and humiliate them. When it came to them sucking my dick, I would make them beg, or say, "Please let me suck your dick." When I was almost finished with them, I'd go back to pounding them in the pussy. I'd push their legs up in the air and I'd pound my dick as hard as I could, trying to hurt them. Finally, I'd cum inside them and all over them. Back then, I'd always release a large amount of cum when it was a rape.

After I was done I'd always be nice. I'd let them put their clothes back on. Sometimes I would tie them up, and sometimes I wouldn't, even though I knew they'd call the police right after I left.

I've often thought about my victims. I wondered what they might have thought or felt while I was raping them. I have no idea. I also wondered what would happen if I saw one of the women I'd raped at a mall or someplace. Would they recognize me? Would they call the police? I'm sure it was hard for them not to change how they viewed and trusted people, especially men, because that's what happened to me when I was raped.

I sometimes wonder whether any of them had bad dreams.

LIFER

IN MANY WAYS, a prison is like a jungle. It's very important to find out quickly which snakes are poisonous, and
which are not. Even more importantly, you need to be sure
your information is accurate. Regardless of the procedures,
there are officers and supervisors who don't like the rules,
and make up their own. For the record, this jail is run by
people, not rules and regulations. The people who work in
jails are, in general, poorly trained, unprofessional, and lazy.

In my opinion, the main reason is this. There are way,
way, way too many Africans working in prisons. In general, people who come to this country from Africa bring
with them experience and observations from their country, where prisoners are treated with a much lower regard
than they are here. For example, I recently heard one of the
African officers say, "If it were up to me, there wouldn't be
any phones in this prison. I have family members at home
in Africa who don't have a phone." I wonder what we can
expect when he becomes a supervisor?

The building I'm in right now, E-block, is always on

lockdown, usually because of fist fights. This building is full of so-called badasses, troublemakers, and just plain jerks! At the moment, everything here in the housing unit seems to be quiet. I don't know how much Family Day (next month) has to do with it. I've heard that all the gangs are at peace until after the Family Day visits are over.

For the last twenty years or so, I've tried to keep to myself. I don't want to get to know people, or talk to them. I'm pretty much a loner, and over the years, I've tried to prevent myself from getting too close to anyone in here. I hate having to deal with losing somebody, or feeling betrayed by them.

I have a particular habit and routine every day. When we're called for chow, I walk alone in the crowd, and I always go to chow hall number 3. I stand in line, wait, move along, get my tray, then I find an empty table and sit down. If anyone wants to sit down and eat with me, fine. If not, that's fine too. I enjoy eating alone.

Not too long ago, a guy who used to live in my block came back to prison. On his first day back, this guy, Nathan, came into chow hall #3, walked up to table I was sitting at, and greeted me as if we were good friends, and fate had brought us back together. Over the next few days, I continued my usual habit, eating alone, and Nathan continued to seek me out. If his tier came into the chow hall before mine and he was already sitting down to eat, I'd go to an empty table. Still, when he saw me, Nathan would leave whatever table he was at, and come to sit with me. Before long, it became a habit, and we ended up eating all our meals together (except breakfast, which I rarely get up for).

Nathan is a likeable guy, but there's no sexual interest (at least, not on my part). We just hit it off. We could talk to each other, and we came to trust each other a little. I never trusted him completely—I don't trust anyone completely—but I think he was willing to trust me. After a while, he bribed the clerk of the housing unit to move his cell closer to mine. When they moved me to a single cell, they moved him in with my ex-cell buddy. We ended up spending more time together on the tier, and in the day room. Nathan, who was a big dude—over six feet tall and 240 lb—would often go outside and work out with weights, but I've never been into that.

In the end, our talking, hanging out and eating together became a "jailhouse friendship." I shouldn't have got into it, but I did. Eventually, I realized I was starting to care about the guy—not in a sexual way, but I looked forward to eating with him, and talking to him. We got along and supported each other. In short, I developed an attachment to him.

Nathan would buy drugs and get high. We didn't talk about it much. He did it when I wasn't around. One morning, around 6 a.m., I heard the sound of the cart that people use when they're packing up to move somewhere. I went to my door and peeped through the window, and I saw Nathan putting his property into a cart with two guards standing watching him. I wanted to yell at him to ask what was going on, but everyone was sleeping so it wouldn't have been cool. I waited until he'd finished packing and he walked past me, pushing the cart. I hollered, "Hey, Nathan, what's going on?" He just looked at me with a blank expression and said, "They're moving me."

Later that day, I found out what happened. Nathan bought some drugs on credit from one of the Muslims. The deadline for paying him back had passed, and Nathan couldn't pay, so, in the chow hall at breakfast, the Muslim hit him in the face. Nathan didn't retaliate, even though he was much bigger than the other guy. Still, he now had all the Muslims in the jail against him, so he asked to be put on protective custody. When you're on P.C. you can't socialize with anyone, and you have to be escorted everywhere in handcuffs. They'll never release Nathan back into population. They'll keep him on P.C., probably for several months, until they move him to another prison, and even there they might keep him on P.C.

There are so many men in these jails over the years that I've cared about, and it always ends up the same way. They leave. Some go home. Some transfer to another prison. Some get in trouble and go on lock-up, or into protective custody. Either way, I'm left feeling the loss. With Nathan, we'd only been close for a short time, but sometimes that doesn't matter. The pain is the same.

This is why I try not to make friends. I don't mean to sound cold, but I don't need them. I have strict standards when it comes to trusting people. I carry myself in such a way as to discourage people from approaching me. By choice, I don't allow people to get close to me. I have very good reasons why I don't want to get close to anyone. As I sit here now, there are 90 men on my tier. I've been here about three months, and I swear, if my life depended on it, I couldn't tell you the names of more than ten guys.

Lately, they've sent out over a hundred guys to other institutions. There's all kinds of stuff going on here that doesn't make any sense. For example, the warden moved all the men in D-Block to E-Block, and those in E-Block to D-Block. These buildings are side by side. No one can come up with any logical reason why they did it. While all these moves were going on, the whole jail was locked down, except for the men that were moving. We're off lockdown now, but they're still moving guys around.

Once I get settled here in my new cell, I'm going to continue writing my story. During a recent meditation, I saw the cover of the book. It was named after was my first Department of Corrections number, given to me in 1962. I was only fifteen years old, the youngest inmate in the state prison system. The title was simply "82189."

In this past week, at least 8 to 10 guys have left the tier and gone to other buildings, or been transferred out of the jail. Likewise, 8 to 10 new guys have moved on to the tier. It's what we call turnover, and it happens a lot. Recently, I made a routine "chronic care" appointment. Long story short, the doctor gave me papers instructing custody to assign me to "single cell status." This changed a lot for me. The cells in the single cell-block are almost twice the size of the cells in the other blocks. I have no idea why, but I appreciate the extra space. I've been feeling lucky and grateful. Hopefully, I'll keep this single cell for a while. My last cell buddy wasn't that bad, although he did (as he put it) hate "queers and faggots." Whadda ya' know!

San Quentin cell

PUBLISHER'S NOTE

The following interview has been edited from Mikita Brottman's correspondence, respectively with Peter Sotos and Chip Smith. A line-break indicates the change in segments.

EXCURSUS

PETER SOTOS:

I'm going to start at the end of your introduction. Though the subject of sympathy is raised well before the end and seems to be where I'm most confounded. I have a feeling that we may feel different forms of sympathy for [Bellows]. There are different forms of sympathy, yes? I think so much of that comes from pinpointing the salient parts; the parts where it might be misunderstood or mispronounced as empathy. Misunderstood again by recognition, projection or titillation?

So, as a question, as a way in, did you feel an obligation towards the sympathy he produced in you? To yourself and/ or to him?

MIKITA BROTTMAN:

I hadn't actually thought much about the question of sympathy until you brought it up here. When writing the introduction, I was thinking closely about the text and how to frame it, assuming most readers would be curious about the broader picture. And in fact, although I do feel sympathy for Henry Bellows, it's sympathy for him as a fellow human being who was sentenced to live a restricted and limited life in unpleasant circumstances. Obviously, he chose to commit his crimes, and did so in full awareness of the pain he was causing and its consequences. But he didn't choose his particular sexual make-up. It was his childhood circumstances (and his father's abuse) that led his sex drive to have such an overpowering influence. There's a point early on in the first section where he sees a woman undressing in a window—this is before he's even started to masturbate—and he says, "I got a hard on just looking... fear was part of the excitement... it felt like Christmas, my birthday, and the Fourth of July all wrapped up into one." There's nothing at all in his life that gives him any sense of self. Then he discovers sexual feelings, and his life is transformed. By the time he goes to prison I think the trajectory of his life is fixed, when it comes to sex at least. That's where I feel sympathy—because he had no choice over the initial formation of his sex drive and its influence over him.

But he's certainly not a likable narrator, and I felt no obligation to him in a personal way. I think the narrative has merit not so much in literary terms, but as a document of evidence. You may feel differently, but I've never read anything by a convicted criminal that is so frank and explicit about the crimes they committed, and the pleasure those crimes gave them. That's what interests me—the frankness, and the lack of any connection between the crimes he perpetrates, and the crimes he's the victim of. Everything else in this line seems to gloss over the acts themselves, decking them out in figurative language, which is a kind of avoidance. Do you know of other autobiographical works that are this honest and forthright? I couldn't find any.

SOTOS: *There's a difference between diaries and literature, of course. But I'm not so sure here either, actually. Off the top of my head, Westley Allan Dodd and Joseph Duncan. Richard Speck gave a hell of an interview that came strongly to my mind as I read Bellows.*

If you don't mind, I'd like to ask you some questions that might be less theoretical. I think you are asking the reader to recognize a sympathy that you can/should guide them to, or am I stuck in a rut there?

BROTTMAN: My assumption is that people who pick up this book are going to be curious about prison life and especially prison sex, and that they're going to be pretty disturbed and maybe disgusted by Bellows. This is someone who's committed horrible crimes, and not only that, but he's completely unapologetic and remorseless, and what he mostly recalls is the pleasure he got from them. In my introduction, I'm hoping to remind the reader that, yes, these are terrible crimes, but this document is a rare opportunity to consider how the perpetrator came to be that way, and to learn about the crimes that were committed against him when he was a child. In other words, to remember that the victim/perpetrator line is not so clear cut.

SOTOS: *I've seen too much writing that seeks to pass child-hood trauma and bad luck or broken trust off as slate for excusing later—sexual—crimes.*

Brottman: But Bellows doesn't make any excuses for his crimes. He doesn't blame anyone. He certainly doesn't blame his childhood trauma. That's what interests me about this document—that he doesn't make the connections that seem so obvious from the outside. He makes no excuses and he's unrepentant.

Sotos: *I have a huge respect for your bullshit detector. Can I ask what put you in prison to—help(?)—these men? Fair to ask if you knew what you were looking for (personally, in light of your greater research) or if it changed as the experience expanded in time? Your background in psychoanalysis, especially in one-to-one situations, as well as your exhaustive work in film studies and criminal forensics leads me to trust this "document" as more yours than the writer's.*

Brottman: It's complicated, but part of the answer is that I feel conscious all the time of the fact that in order for our day-to-day lives to continue placidly and calmly, all the horror, cruelty, violence and torture has to be kept out of sight. Most of it stays hidden in institutions like prisons, slaughterhouses, hospitals, psych facilities, children's homes and assisted living facilities. I know I feel a strong drive to find out what goes on in places like that not only because repression of those horrors makes my placid daily life possible, but because people in those facilities are essentially no different from me. And of all those facilities and institutions, prison was the most accessible. The more I learned about the prison system, the more interested I became. It's like a parallel underground world containing millions of people, with its own schools, hospitals, government, etc.

I never set out to help, teach, influence, or advise. I just get interested in something. And when I'm really interested and engaged and involved, the other things come from it. The best teachers, therapists, and advisors (in my experience) are those who are deeply engrossed and involved in whatever the subject happens to be. I became compelled and fascinated by those men in prison living in this strange parallel world.

I think this document helps us remember that the victim/perpetrator line is not so clear cut, and that "sex" in a coercive context is a complicated thing. I think it also gives us a glimpse at the kind of life we don't often get to see. I'm fascinated by Bellows' experiences, and I think it's difficult to draw a line between being curious in a sort of detached, voyeuristic way, and curious in a way that helps us learn, understand and sympathize. I think one leads to the other. I'm hoping people will pick up the book from prurient curiosity, and come to understand more about what goes on in prison, and the complexities of sex in that context. I don't know if that answers your question or not.

Sotos: I think I have to work a bit to have it remain a document here since you added an introduction and I'm far more interested in what you have to say about it being an actual document. You felt it had enough merit on its own to, what, only make you want to know more? Or explaining it for the people who are curious but to a degree that doesn't match your own?

Brottman: I thought it needed putting in context—I wanted to give readers a sense of how I came to know Bellows and a bit more about his life and his situation when I met him. Do I think the text would stand on its own? Maybe, but I think it's more interesting this way. The introduction is meant to be a sort of guidepost for orientation, not a map of the territory.

Sotos: *You like that Bellows doesn't make any excuses for his crimes and yet you make a point of where exactly you think his sex life was fixed—fixated?—and that it came from abuse. Maybe a bit of an excuse there?*

Brottman: There's a difference between an explanation/ understanding and an excuse. You can understand the cause and origin of a person's actions without forgiving or excusing them. I think what Bellows did was terrible, but I understand why and how he came to be that way.

Sotos: *Do you think turning into what he became, sexually, is a legitimate—read helpful, healthful—response?*

Brottman: By "what he became, sexually," do you mean a rape victim, a "prison bitch," a rapist, or all of it? I don't think it's a question of a "healthy response." There's no alternative. It's like one of those experiments Harlow did with baby monkeys. If you put a baby monkey in total isolation for six months, it's going to come out socially damaged and in a state of emotional shock. It might rock, it might gnaw on its own body, it might stop eating. There is no "healthy response" in a situation like that, only different kinds of reactions to the trauma.

I feel as if I'm not answering your questions because you're trying to get at something else, like why am I interested in this guy, and why do I want to see this story published, and what's my personal investment in it, and is my own interest in it healthy, or something like that. I'm curious that you're more interested in the intro than the story. Could you say a bit more about why that is?

SOTOS: I was thinking that the complexities of sex are more central to literature and the complexities of the prison system more attuned to polemical arguments for change and greater sympathy. It's those complexities, the blurred lines, that give the book merit to me—above and beyond the life poor Bellows lived. And I think your background on Bellows is essential. Therefore, I'm comfortable saying your interest in him is of more concern to me than the example he might otherwise be of a harsh life badly figured and reconnoitered.

Using Harlow is a great way to lead (lob?) but I think we read him differently. Why, for example, and to badly paraphrase Harlow, give the monkeys the benefit of the doubt? They were animals and tortured in beautifully imagined and constructed devices. Add science and peer review. Animals that were incapable of expressing the suppositions and details Harlow was seeking to test. The problem, here, in applying the comparison is that we'd be looking for one monkey to be especially interesting beyond instinct. Are you talking about instinct? An instinctual response to trauma?

Maybe John Money's messes are more applicable?

BROTTMAN: I think we agree that the interest and merit of the book is in the way it allows the blurriness of those lines to be foregrounded, more than anything else. This story shows that voyeuristic, prurient, intrusive curiosity overlaps with an "objective" therapeutic desire to learn, help, nurture, understand, etc. And in a similar way, it shows us that one way people respond to trauma is by absorbing, colonizing, and ultimately fetishizing it, and this is in fact as "normal" and natural as becoming averse, phobic, isolated, asexual, or any of the other familiar reactions so often reiterated in the media.

Another thing I forgot to mention about the manuscript is how it approaches the question of gender. When we read about the way Bellows "became a woman," it really shines a new light on the idea of gender fluidity. Bellows "transitioned" gender, but he was physically forced to do so by acts of violence. That doesn't mean he didn't later come to embrace that identity. Then to repudiate it. I think the thing I like best about the document is the way it foregrounds the puritanism, narrowness and privilege of much liberal thinking.

About Harlow, yes, instinct. I'm saying that Bellows' response to trauma is as natural and instinctive as a love-deprived monkey gnawing on its own limb.

CHIP SMITH:

I'm curious about the stark shift in tone and narrative texture that occurs between what we can refer to as Bellows' "youth memoir" (i.e., "Defective Delinquent") and the fragmentary entries that follow. It's really quite striking to me—like another voice takes over, or a voice removed from what it describes—and the point of demarcation might be the gang rape, if that's not too tidily story-driven to suspect. In your introduction, you suggest that Bellows intended to flesh out these segments to bring them into step with his established autobiographical flow, but I'm not so sure this would have come to pass. To push a bit further, I sense a bright-line breakdown in introspective capacity, and to me this is perhaps the most salient aspect of the text considered as a kind of psychological artifact—that the shift might unwittingly reveal a schism in reflective self-apprehension, where the nuance of a sifted childhood memory gives way to the superficial anecdote of remorseless criminality. So I'm curious about your read on this observation, beginning with whether you think it's mistaken. And on the assumption there's something worth exploring, what's your interpretation?

MIKITA BROTTMAN:

I think you're spot-on. The gang rape is the clear-cut division, the ritual of initiation into another life, and another perspective. I agree that I can't imagine Bellows doing much to revise these sections. If there were more memories to include, he would have included them. He might have refined the prose a little, but I don't think he would have made substantial changes. In "Defective Delinquent," he returns to see the world from the perspective of a child (sensations of arousal are called "funny feelings"; he doesn't know what "incorrigible" means, etc.). In the later chapters, even when he's recalling events that happened when he was still a young teenager (he's only 14 when the gang rape occurs), he suddenly has an adult mindset. Very soon after the gang-rape, he's writing from the perspective of a jaded adult ("It was a turn-on to have guys watching me suck dick"), as if that trauma caused a schism in his self-perception.

I hesitate to bring up a Freudian idea, knowing how unfashionable he is (and I feel Henry Bellows turning in his grave), but the concept of what Freud called *nachträglich* (usually translated as "afterwardness") seems too apposite to ignore. It's the idea of deferred action, "the pathogenic effect of a traumatic event occurring in childhood... [manifesting] retrospectively when the child reaches a subsequent phase of sexual development." In other words, the effects of a trauma can be deferred, but when they manifest, they have the same effect as they would if they'd only just happened. So just as the gang-rape fast-forwarded Bellows into jaded adulthood, so writing about the gang-rape causes him to fast-forward into a present-day point-of-view, casting him immediately out of that childhood perspective and into that of his current self—a cynical lifer in his seventies who's learned to take pleasure in his own servitude and humiliation. Freud says something similar about a patient's feeling for his father: "As long as his father was alive it showed itself in unmitigated rebelliousness and open discord, but immediately after his death it took the form of a neurosis based on abject submission and deferred obedience to him." Bellows fights against his father, but as soon as his father is out of the picture (after the gang rape), Bellows turns into a submissive rape victim, just like his mother. At the same time, the narrative voice jumps forward from child to adult, appropriating the father's cynical worldliness.

SMITH: Whether via Freudian overlay or through the sympathetic reading of a life history in outline, the temptation to explain and contextualize criminal behavior weighs upon our interpretation. This might be useful and good in some respects, but we also know that Bellows' father was a rapist. If granular accounts of causative or formative experiences—whether scaffolded by psychoanalytic theory or some perfect storm of sociological conditions—inform our understanding of crime and deviance in a particular case study, do we run the risk of ignoring the possibility of a deeper script? Behavior genetics may be informative here, and we all remember what happened with Norman Mailer's pet. Not that I expect you to disentangle the multiplex interplay of nature and environment in present context, but I am curious as to your views as an interdisciplinary psychologist with frontline experience. Suppose Henry had been adopted into a healthier family environment? Would there be, to borrow his line, "no story to tell"? Or would it be a different version of the same story?

BROTTMAN: In the first part of the memoir, Bellows mentions a brother and a sister, both significantly younger than himself. I'm not sure what happened to the brother, or whether the parents divorced or stayed together, but I know he kept in contact with the sister who, from what I'm aware, led an ordinary, law-abiding life. Perhaps the family environment changed. Maybe the other kids were treated differently. Either way, I don't think it was genetics that led to his sexually coercive behavior (although it clearly primed him), it was his childhood maltreatment—not just his father's beatings, but witnessing his father's abuse of his mother (maybe finding it arousing), and then, most significantly, the traumatic gang rape. If he'd been adopted into a hypothetical loving family, he'd probably have still been a troubled and troublemaking kid, and it was his troublemaking that got him into the prison system and led to the gang rape. On the other hand, if he'd been treated with more consideration by his family and by the cops, and if he'd been encouraged in some area of expression that allowed him to develop a healthy sense of self and dispel his pent-up energy in competition—baseball, martial arts, football, wrestling— he could probably have lived a much more satisfying life.

As far as I'm aware, he fathered no children himself, which is probably a good thing.

SMITH: Circling back to your exchange with Pete, I do think it's interesting to view Bellows' text in light of recent cultural trends, and particularly with regard to evolving concepts of gender. I happened to read 82189 around the same time I read Andrea Long Chu's Females: A Concern and I couldn't help but be struck by the contextual resonance of her concept of "femaleness" as a kind of chimerical existential passivity—as a universal psychic state that emerges in abeyance to external desire. While a gang rape initiation might seem radically different from Long Chu's immersive experience with "sissy porn," the results are curiously similar. One way to put it might be that what for Bellows was a matter of survival was for Long Chu a matter of actualization, but the idea of a kind of internal plasticity—or "fluidity," as they say—of the self sort of coheres, or at least invites exploration.

BROTTMAN: I'm not sure I agree with the parallel, though I don't know Long Chu's work. I think that, up until a certain age—maybe 15 or 16—our sexuality is plastic in the sense that the unconscious will work to colonize a traumatic experience into something sexual, even if the traumatic experience itself isn't a sexual one, as with the child subject to humiliating punishment in childhood who, as an adult, has a strong predilection for masochism. I think it's very, very difficult after the age of 15 or 16—maybe even impossible—to change what one responds to, sexually. To use a cliché, men in prison or on board ship may indulge in "situational homosexuality," but those who are straight will be fantasizing about women, or will return to women when the opportunity arises, or will select a highly feminized male partner (a "prison bitch" like Bellows). When Bellows came to find his abjection pleasurable, it wasn't because his basic sexuality had been transformed and he was now a man who preferred "sucking dick" (as he puts it), but because "sucking dick" felt shameful, and shame turned him on because his sexuality was fundamentally masochistic. Mostly, he played the submissive role. But when he got the chance (with his victims), he played the dominant role. Both are manifestations of the same dynamic. In other words, if we find something sexually pleasurable in a new encounter (a new kind of porn, sex act, fantasy etc.), it's because it's not really new—we've just found something in it that fits our particular script.

SMITH: *I think this context-dependent dynamic is actually close to what I have in mind with the perhaps ill-advised comparison to Andrea Long Chu's provocations. I see the toggling roles of victim and perpetrator playing out within the same role-fixated inner drama, like plotting the dimensions of a cordoned space. We've discussed the general absence of empathy and introspection that characterizes Bellows' account of his "role" as a sexual predator, but what do you make of the singular arguable deviation, where he's given to wonder about his victims' dreams?*

BROTTMAN: I'm not sure it's a deviation. He says, "I've often thought about my victims," but everything he mentions refers not so much to them, but to his role in their lives. Would they call the cops if they saw him, would they recognize him, did they stop trusting men, etc. Wondering whether they had bad dreams is another way of wondering if they dreamed about him, or if his assault had an impact even on their dreams. He wants to know the effect he had on them, whether it was permanent, whether it reached their unconscious, whether he left them permanently changed. That's my reading.

SMITH: *Another script we're familiar with—in this case a cultural script—concerns the current iteration of "true crime" melodrama, which is now largely relegated to podcasts and TV documentaries that focus on forensics and suburban outcry. On first impression, a raw text like 82189* *would seem to grate against the spirit and appeal of this genre.*

BROTTMAN: I don't think the "true crime" audience (mostly women) would have any interest in this text. It's not really "crime" they're interested in, but a very particular type of crime presented from a very particular perspective (that of the martyr-victim, their families, police, prosecution). There's no place in the "true crime" genre for the perpetrator's perspective. And a violent rapist? Forget it. That's why I just can't get into most "true crime" podcasts, documentaries, etc. It's all about the female victims (despite the fact that all perpetrators begin as victims, too). It's all so superficial and sanctimonious. One of the things that interested me about Bellows' manuscript is that it's a crime story from the perpetrator's perspective. Those are very rare. Well-written, thoughtful ones are unheard of. The only exception I've ever been able to find is Nathan Leopold's memoir, *Life Plus 99 Years*. He doesn't write about the crime, but that's understandable.

SMITH: *In Thirteen Girls you present a series of fictionalized vignettes centered around the victims of real-life serial killers. It's a fascinating book for so many reasons, but as a study of what you refer to in your coda as "the afterlife of murder through the eyes of the people it has affected" I think it's worth revisiting in qualified relation to 82189. Bellows wasn't a serial killer, of course, but he was a perpetrator as well as a victim of horrific crimes—and his story, recorded without fictional conceit, is in a sense about aftermath, or traumatic sequelae, albeit from a different perspective. I suppose there is also the matter of your empathic investment in these differently situated narratives, the looming sense that you could have been a victim?*

BROTTMAN: Yes, I'm interested in the parts of crime stories that don't get any attention. These include the impact of the crime on the victims' friends and family members, as well as those more on the periphery of the victims' lives. These ideas are at the heart of my two most recent books as well. *An Unexplained Death* is, in part, an extended essay about missing people, emphasizing that often, people aren't missed or mourned as much as we like to think they are. *Couple Found Slain*, which comes out in June 2021, is about a guy who killed his parents and has been in a psych hospital for the last thirty years, despite recovering from paranoid schizophrenia. I like thinking around the crime, underneath and on the edges, studying the fallout that's usually overlooked because it doesn't usually interest people.

I do sometimes think that I could have been a victim of crime—I did a lot of hitchhiking alone when I was at college—but I also think that it was equally likely that I could have been a perpetrator. So yes, empathy all round, there but for the grace of god, etc. I was at a parole hearing today and I certainly had a lot more sympathy for the inmate, who'd been in prison for thirty years, than for the victim's family representative, who barely remembered the victim.

SMITH: *I think it's to Bellows' credit that he doesn't really promote a reformist agenda, yet it's impossible to* read his memoir without being confronted by the brutal reality of prison rape. It might be argued that things have improved in the decades since he was first assaulted and "turned out," but the underlying issue remains somewhat taboo, with dismissive jokes often being the first response when the subject is raised. The persistence of what might be characterized as motivated ignorance on this front is perhaps especially striking when it's considered against the prevailing cultural backdrop, where we find—in the #MeToo movement, most conspicuously—a mood of heightened sensitivity to the broader societal problem of sexual violence. What do you think accounts for this apparent dissonance?

BROTTMAN: People on the outside don't really care about prison inmates. They're invisible in the media and cultural landscape. Prison itself is debated, of course, and policy related to crime and criminal sentencing, but inmates are invisible because they have no voice, no access to the media, no cultural role. The common assumption is that by breaking the law, they've given up the right to be included in the conversation, and—to a degree—they get what they deserve. I think there's a sense that prison rape isn't "real" rape because no one in prison is "innocent," and in an all-male environment, there's no alternative than for men to have sex with each other. Rape is regarded as a sort of "breaking in."

In relation to the question of victims and empathy, we like to believe that victims are "undeserving, innocent" people and perpetrators are "evil" and deserve to be punished. Whereas in fact, victim and perpetrator are different points on the spectrum in a person's life. Most perpetrators were once victims themselves. It just depends at what point in their lives you're choosing to tell the story. That's my problem with "true crime," in a nutshell.

SMITH: *This may come off as sanctimonious, but it is possible that the publication of 82189 could raise awareness about sexual victimization behind bars. Can you provide an overview of the relevant data, and your views on how the problem should be addressed?*

BROTTMAN: I don't really have any special knowledge about this, and I don't trust statistics or generalizations. In short, I think that to address prison rape, society would have to address the question of all the other horrors that go on in prison, and that's not going to happen. It's the constant repression of those horrors that makes it possible for us to believe (as with #MeToo) that sexual abuse is an aberration, rather than the norm.

MIKITA BROTTMAN is a writer, lecturer, and psychoanalyst who lives in Baltimore. She is the author of numerous books, including *An Unexplained Death* (2018) and *Couple Found Slain* (2021, both Henry Holt & Co.).

PETER SOTOS is a Chicago-based writer and artist best known for his psycho-literary studies of crime, pornography, and aesthetics. He is the author, most recently, of *Ingratitude* (2018, Nine-Banded Books).

CHIP SMITH is the founder and managing editor of Nine-Banded Books.

HENRY BELLOWS is the pen-name of an American writer and prisoner who died in 2018. *82189: Confessions of a Prison Bitch* has been published posthumously in accordance with his wishes.

Caveat Lector.

www.NineBandedBooks.com